FDIC DIRECTOR SUITS: LESSONS LEARNED

SECOND EDITION

AMERICAN ASSOCIATION OF BANK DIRECTORS

DAVID BARIS
President
American Association of Bank Directors

LOYAL HORSLEY
Associate
BuckleySandler LLP

1

FDIC Director Suits: Lessons Learned

Second Edition

2015

Copyright ©

American Association of Bank Directors

All Rights Reserved

American Association of Bank Directors
National Capital Office
1250 24th Street, NW, Suite 700
Washington, DC 20037

www.AABD.org

ISBN-13: 978-1511716277

ISBN-10: 1511716274

WHAT BANK DIRECTORS CAN LEARN FROM FDIC SUITS AGAINST DIRECTORS OF FAILED BANKS

SECOND EDITION

TABLE OF CONTENTS

5

INTRODUCTION AND SUMMARY

The American Association of Bank Directors has undertaken a review of the FDIC's civil suits against directors of failed banks and savings institutions to find out what directors of open banks can learn from the one hundred and four suits (involving more than 793 directors and officers) filed from July 2010 through January 12, 2015.[1]

We undertook this study primarily to assist AABD members and others who currently serve as bank directors in avoiding the fate of those who have been sued.[2] Studies on the causes of bank failures and what can be learned from them are plentiful for the failures of banks and savings and loan associations during the S&L crisis of the late 1980's and early 1990's, but not for the more recent failures. A bibliography of many of the earlier studies and a few more recent studies is provided in Appendix I.

---

[1] The FDIC has authorized suits against 148 failed institutions and 1,181 individual defendants. Federal Deposit Insurance Corporation, *Professional Liability Lawsuits, available at* http://www.fdic.gov/bank/individual/failed/pls/ (last visited January 12, 2015). 502 financial institutions have failed since August 1, 2008. Federal Deposit Insurance Corporation, *Failed Bank List*, http://www.fdic.gov/bank/individual/failed/banklist.html (last visited February 2, 2015).

[2] For comparison, nearly 25% of the total institutions during the savings and loan crisis subject to FDIC authority resulted in lawsuits, while only 104 suits have been filed out of the 502 bank failures, or about 20%. However, if the additional 45 lawsuits that have been authorized are combined with the 104 filed suits, the percentage is nearly 30% (149 out of 502).

7

Many of the complaints are not drafted in a way that provides clear guidance to those who wish to learn from them. Some make assertions that require bank directors to be clairvoyant, all-knowing or all-powerful in identifying, fixing or avoiding problems – clearly skill sets not required for bank directors to meet their fiduciary duties. There is no guidance AABD can provide that would help bank directors become clairvoyant or control events outside their control or never to make a mistake in judgment.

The complaints do not provide clarity on how the state standard of care would apply to a bank director based on a particular set of facts. State standards of care fall into simple or ordinary negligence standards and gross negligence standards.[3] Many of the complaints allege simple or ordinary negligence, gross negligence and breach of fiduciary duty without differentiating what actions or inactions may have caused the director to commit one or all of those standards or defining what those standards are. The complaints allege ordinary negligence even where the standard of care in a state in which the failed bank was based was, AABD believes, gross negligence. The complaints never acknowledge the Business Judgment Rule under which courts allow directors a wide range of discretion and judgment, or differentiate between the decision-making process of the board from the decision itself. Many complaints fault directors for making decisions that did not work out.

---

[3] Bank Director Standards of Care and Protections – a Fifty-State Survey, David Baris, Ed., 2013

It is for those reasons that this Report recommends that bank directors aim high; that is, they should not rely on a gross negligence standard of care even though that may be the applicable standard in their state. And they should not rely on the protection of the Business Judgment Rule.

One major finding in this Report is that bank directors are at higher risk of potential personal liability if they approve individual loans than if they do not. Almost all of the complaints assert that directors, as members of the board of directors or a director loan committee, approved loans on which their bank suffered losses, and that the loans should not have been made. The complaints suggest that bank directors who approve loans are held to the standard of a professional lending officer or credit officer. The complaints can be read to suggest that a director is at risk of being held legally responsible for losses on loans if there is a flaw in the loan analysis or in the appraisal, a "red flag" that the board or board committee should have inquired about but didn't, or similar mistakes that bank boards of directors rely reasonably on bank loan and credit officers to identify for the board and correct.

As a consequence, the Report recommends that bank directors, as board or board committee members, stop approving individual loans other than those required by law to be approved by a board or board committee. At the federal level, only loans subject to Regulation O are required to be approved by a bank board of directors.

AABD has previously requested that the FDIC approve a "safe harbor" for directors on boards or board committees that approve or ratify loans, but the FDIC has refused. The FDIC also disagrees with AABD's advice to bank directors not to approve individual loans because the FDIC believes that bank directors of community banks who know the community and the people who reside or do business there can add value by reviewing and approving loans. AABD agrees that community bank directors can add value, but not at the price of elevating potential personal liability. Once the FDIC approves a safe harbor for directors who act in good faith and without personal conflict in approving individual loans, AABD will withdraw its recommendation. See Appendices III and IV for AABD's correspondence with the FDIC.

Even if bank directors do not approve loans, they are still susceptible to potential lawsuits if their bank fails. This study will summarize the other bases that the FDIC has used to sue directors of failed banks and recommendations on how directors might minimize potential liability and risk of suit by the FDIC.

The FDIC complaints make allegations against outside directors that implicitly require board members to have skills that many do not currently possess. While the federal banking agencies do not have regulations requiring (with one exception) bank directors to have specific training or background prior to assuming their positions or require any ongoing training, AABD believes that bank directors need to do so in order to mitigate risks of personal liability. Such training may provide additional skills to bank directors to help avoid actions by their banks that might later be used as a basis of personal liability. The OCC has adopted a guideline in the form of a regulation that

10

requires formal training for boards of directors of national and federal savings banks with assets of $50 billion or more, and certain foreign banks doing business in the U.S.

AABD provides the tools by which bank directors can become better prepared to mitigate personal liability risks and become more valuable board members over matters that they can control. Among the resources offered to AABD members is a six hour core course specially designed for outside board members conducted on bank premises or other location designated by the board of directors. Details of the core course and AABD's Bank Director Certification Program are available on its website at www.aabd.org.

AmTrust, a D&O insurer, has agreed to provide credits of up to 15% on D&O insurance for qualified banks whose directors participate in the Bank Director Certification Program.

AABD also offers independent assessments of bank boards of directors that provide recommendations on how to minimize personal liability risks and improve board and board committee governance.

AABD has evaluated the 1992 FDIC Statement on the Duties and Responsibilities of Bank Directors and Officers ("1992 FDIC Statement" or "Statement"). Although the 1992 FDIC Statement, in our view, is outdated and woefully inadequate, the FDIC continues to rely heavily on it to help decide whether to approve and file civil suits against directors and officers of failed banks. In that light, it is essential for current bank directors to familiarize themselves with the language in the 1992 FDIC Statement and attempt to conduct their business in a manner that will be consistent with the standards set forth in the 1992 FDIC Statement. See Appendix II for a copy of the FDIC Statement.

In a related report, AABD summarizes the standards of care applicable to bank directors in all fifty states, the Business Judgment Rule applicable in each state, and the authority for bank directors to rely reasonably on the information and opinions of bank management, outside advisors, and board committees in making decisions.[4]

The following section is a summary of the most common elements found in the FDIC's complaints. AABD then summarizes the provisions of the 1992 FDIC Statement pertaining to bank directors, followed by a set of recommendations to directors of open banks and savings institutions designed to avoid or minimize personal liability that can grow out of these suits. These recommendations should not be interpreted as requirements for bank directors to meet their fiduciary duties. Finally, this Report summarizes each of the one hundred and four suits filed against directors of failed banks and savings institutions since July 2010 (through January 12, 2015).

---

[4] Id.

COMMON ALLEGATIONS IN FDIC COMPLAINTS

The following is a summary of the most common allegations identified in the FDIC complaints. It should be noted that all but three of the lawsuits filed to date have been filed against community bank directors. Only Washington Mutual and IndyMac were large institutions and only director-officers were sued in those two cases.

Loan Underwriting Policies and Procedures

One of the most commonly cited allegations in the complaints was the lack of proper oversight and adequate policies regarding the loan underwriting process. Specifically, missing documentation of borrower income and credit worthiness was used to support a negligence theory of liability. Collateral valuation was another issue cited in most of the complaints where collateral was purportedly overvalued, not appraised until after the loans were funded, or was not sufficient to cover the loan amounts dispersed. There were many issues with perfecting security interests in collateral because policies did not require staff to submit perfected security agreements at closing. High loan-to-value ratios were very commonly cited as an inherent problem with lending practices. These claims were made against inside and outside directors equally. Most of the claims related to the loss loans that individual directors personally approved.

More often than not, the failed bank had a written loan policy that regulators deemed adequate, but that the directors did not follow. The loan policies usually covered required documentation, underwriting procedures, permissible LTV ratios, and the maximum loan amount that could be approved without the board loan committee's involvement.

Most of the complaints assume that directors who approved loans as members of the board or a board committee should have independently investigated loans presented by management for board approval to make certain the loans were underwritten properly, as if they were loan officers themselves and had no loan or credit officers who had reviewed the loans prior to the submission of the loans to the board or board committee.[5]

Most of the complaints cited deficient loan administration and underwriting practices (e.g., using interest reserves for problem loans, poor appraisal practices, or not having updated financial information and updated appraisals at the time of origination or renewal, modification or extension).

Loan Approvals by the Board of Directors and/or a Board Loan Committee

Nearly all of the complaints brought against directors list individual loans on which the failed bank

---

[5] The complaints typically cite deficiencies in the loan underwriting, credit administration, loan policies or in compliance with such policies, violations of law or regulation or violations of safe and sound lending practices for which the board member is held accountable even though the work in preparing the documentation and recommendations was done by professional lenders and credit officers.

suffered losses. These loans were either approved or ratified by the board of directors, or the loans were approved by the bank loan committee that consisted of officers and directors. Twenty-six (26) complaints did not list any outside directors and were brought either against officers or director-officers only.

About ninety percent of the complaints were filed against directors who approved or ratified individual loans that suffered losses; the strong impression is left that board members who did not approve or ratify individual loans were generally not sued or were at a much lower risk of being sued. Note, however, that directors who were not present during approvals of loss loans or who abstained from votes on particular loss loans were sometimes named in complaints.

Ratification is an after-the-fact affirmation. By the time the ratification is made, the bank has a legal obligation to make the loan and in most cases has already funded the loan. But our reading of the FDIC complaints suggests that the FDIC makes no distinction between approval and ratification as to the potential liability of a bank director.

Most of the complaints asserted that the bank and its board or board loan committee violated loan policies, procedures and regulations. If the board or board committee approved or ratified loans, the board or board committee members appear to be held to the same standard of knowledge and skills that would apply to a professional lender.

Lack of Separation Between the Lending and Credit Function

Many loans were analyzed by the same loan officers who originated the loans; in other words, there was a lack of separation between the loan origination function and the credit underwriting and administration function. This led to a lack of internal quality control to make independent assessments regarding the safety of loans. In some complaints, the credit officer was deemed to lack independence because he or she reported to the Chief Lending Officer or Chief Executive Officer who had lending authority.

Approximately 70% of the complaints asserted that there was a lack of sufficient independence of the credit from the lending origination function.

Concentration of ADC or CRE Loans and Loans to Small Groups of Borrowers

Another common element cited in the complaints was the concentration of loans in either a small group of borrowers, in a specific geographic area, or a high concentration of ADC and CRE loans. In roughly a quarter of the complaints, the FDIC cited bank concentration of loans to a small pool of borrowers. For example, one bank had a group of 10 large borrowers that represented nearly 100% of bank capital to loan ratio. In all but four complaints, the concentration of ADC and CRE loans was cited as dangerously high. This concentration was always compared to peer groups and the concentrations cited in bank regulatory guidance. In all the complaints that listed ADC and CRE loan concentrations as a problem, the percentage of ADC/CRE loans to capital was substantially more than the peer group average or the regulatory guidance limit recommended (often ADC/CRE loans were well over 700% of the bank's capital before the bank's closing).

Many of the complaints cited continuing ADC/CRE lending in late 2006 and later in face of national, regional and local real estate markets weakening.

All but three of the complaints cited insufficient risk management systems to address loan concentrations.

Offering a New Financial Product or Entering New Geographic Markets

A small number of the complaints cited the board's failure to properly plan for the offering of new financial products or entering new geographic markets. The FDIC claimed that the failed banks took excessive risks without implementing protections or hiring experienced employees. About a third of the complaints took issue with the concentration of loans in certain local geographic areas known to be experiencing a real estate market decline. At the same time, some complaints noted the making of loans outside the bank's core area as an issue because of the lack of familiarity with economic trends outside the bank's traditional lending area.

Incompetent or Inexperienced Management

Approximately 65% of the complaints state that the directors did not ensure that the bank had competent and sufficient personnel in place to engage in the lending activities in which the bank was engaged.

Excessive Growth Strategies During Challenging Economy

About half the complaints asserted that boards created strategies that encouraged growth rates and excessive loan originations. The FDIC often cited stated goals that included boards acknowledging financial problems but deciding to attempt to "grow out" of the issues. Most banks wanted to gain market share and did so by encouraging rapid growth in generating high-risk loans, either in the ADC/CRE sector or through the use of "creative" financing such as adjustable rate or subprime mortgages. Moreover, the incentives sometimes created by rewarding loan officers for generating these loans compounded the problems because it led to more high-risk loans.

Approximately 65% of the complaints criticized board members for permitting the bank to grow rapidly, in many cases based on the use of non-core liabilities and brokered deposits.

Approximately 80% of the complaints asserted that board members failed to follow economic conditions either at all or not sufficiently, and didn't document those efforts or change the bank's lending as a result.

About 20% claimed board members should have known as early as August 2006 that continued underwriting of ADC/CRE loans was imprudent because the market was overheated.

Compensation Systems that Incentivize the Taking of Unreasonable Risk

Some complaints alleged conflicts of interest in the bank's compensation structures because loan officers were awarded for originating new loans whether or not the loans were high quality. Most of the time, loan officers' compensation were not adversely affected by having originated loans on which the bank suffered losses. The compensation systems were usually cited as exacerbating the problems of irresponsible and excessive growth strategies.

Approximately 40% of the complaints claimed that incentive compensation rewarded loan officers for volume without consideration of the quality of loans.

Insider Loans and Illegal or Imprudent Use of Bank Funds

In about a quarter of the complaints, the FDIC cited the board's approval of either illegal or fiscally imprudent use of bank funds to support a breach of fiduciary duty claim. For example, in one complaint the bank authorized dividend payments based on false profitability numbers created by using interest reserves to show profits. In another, the bank paid dividends to its holding company when it was illegal under state law to do so. Further, loans made to directors or officers were often cited by the FDIC. One bank gave preferential treatment to a group of board members who used the funds in a failed business venture. Finally, the use of bank funds for personal expenses was noted in at least two complaints as a breach of fiduciary duty. For example, a donation was made to an event that was the wedding of a board member. Excessive use of funds for director meetings in exotic and luxurious locations was cited as wasteful spending.

Directors Ignored or Refused to Follow Regulators' Suggestions and Warnings

Virtually all of the FDIC complaints assert that banking agencies issued warnings and recommendations in multiple reports of examination that were ultimately not heeded. The most common warnings were the high concentration of ADC/CRE loans, improper underwriting policies, lack of internal controls and oversight over lending, use of brokered deposits, and improper use of interest reserves to support loan financing. The complaints use the lack of effective action in response to these warnings that put the board on notice as representing gross negligence. The argument was that because the directors knew that their policies were adverse to a safe and conservative growth strategy and sound underwriting procedures, the boards and officers acted recklessly.

Standard of Care Asserted in Complaints

In most cases, the FDIC complaints assert claims for both simple and gross negligence. In addition, they generally assert breach of fiduciary duties without specifying whether the breach is based on simple or gross negligence.

As explained in the next section, the U.S. Supreme Court decided in 1995 that the FDIC's claim that there was a simple negligence common law standard applicable to bank directors was wrong. Instead, the Court ruled that a federal statute applies a gross negligence standard as defined by state law unless the state has a more stringent standard (simple negligence), in which case the FDIC may sue on that standard.

As previously mentioned, AABD has issued a report on the standard of care in each of the fifty states. Our reading suggests that the vast majority of the states have adopted a gross negligence standard of care, whether directly through statutory provisions, or through courts applying the Business Judgment Rule. Nevertheless, the FDIC complaints in states where a gross negligence standard has been adopted often include a simple negligence claim.

THE 1992 FDIC STATEMENT

The 1992 FDIC Statement on the Duties and Responsibilities of Bank Directors and Officers sets forth the FDIC's expectations of outside directors and the standards by which it evaluates whether to sue outside directors.

The FDIC states that directors are responsible for the following:

- Selecting, monitoring, and evaluating competent management;
- Establishing business strategies and policies;
- Monitoring and assessing the progress of business operations;
- Establishing and monitoring adherence to policies and procedures required by statute, regulation, and principles of safety and soundness; and
- Making business decisions on the basis of fully informed and meaningful deliberation

According to the 1992 FDIC Statement, directors must require timely and ample information to discharge board responsibilities. Directors are also responsible for requiring management to respond promptly to supervisory criticism.

The FDIC states that it "will not bring civil suits against directors . . . who fulfill their responsibilities, including the duties of loyalty and care, and who make reasonable business judgments on a fully informed basis and after proper deliberation."

The 1992 FDIC Statement also summarizes the nature of the suits filed by the FDIC against directors, which includes cases:

- where the director engaged in dishonest conduct or approved or condoned abusive transactions with insiders;
- where a director was responsible for the failure of an institution to adhere to applicable laws and regulations, its own policies, or any agreement with a supervisory authority or where the director otherwise participated in a safety or soundness violation; or
- where directors failed to establish proper underwriting policies and to monitor adherence thereto, or approved loans that they knew or had reason to know were improperly underwritten, or where the board failed to heed warnings from regulators or professional advisors

The 1992 FDIC Statement recognizes that one of the factors considered in determining whether to bring an action against a director is the distinction between inside and outside directors. Outside directors generally do not participate in the conduct of the day-to-day business operations of the bank. The most common suits brought against outside directors, according to the Statement, either involve insider abuse or situations where the director failed to heed warnings from regulators, accountants, attorneys or others that there was a significant problem in the bank which required correction.

Although the Statement recognizes the distinction between outside and inside directors and between outside directors and management, it is not entirely consistent in that distinction. For example, it identifies lawsuits related to directors approving loans that "they knew or had reason to know were improperly underwritten." But when boards and board committees do approve loans (and many community bank boards and board loan committees do so even though not required to do so), they typically are not supplanting the loan and credit officers who previously reviewed the loans in depth and recommended approval, or the officer loan committee that might have recommended approval, but rather their review is a high level review of whether the loan should be made consistent with the overall strategy of the bank.

The Statement also fails to acknowledge the Business Judgment Rule, which in many states means that the board members are protected from personal liability if they exercised their business judgment in good faith and without a conflict of interest. Nor does it recognize that directors may reasonably rely on the work of officers and employees, advisors, and board committees in reaching decisions such as whether to approve a loan, set policy and risk tolerances, and adopt internal controls and systems.

FDIC used to believe that the applicable standard of care for bank directors was simple negligence based on federal common law. However, the U.S. Supreme Court ruled in the mid-1990's that the FDIC and RTC were incorrect; the standard of care is gross negligence unless the law of the state where the failed institution was based has a more stringent standard.

In its 1997 Annual Report, the FDIC stated that regardless of state law, it will not sue a director unless the director committed gross negligence, although the FDIC will assert a simple negligence count in suits involving failed banks in states that have a simple negligence standard. Because this policy was adopted following the adoption of the 1992 FDIC Statement, it is not reflected in that statement.

The 1992 FDIC Statement states that directors need to be "fully informed" prior to making decisions or else they might be in breach of their fiduciary duties. This is not an accurate statement of the law in most, if not all jurisdictions. Directors should be sufficiently informed of material facts or reasonably rely on others to enable them to make a reasonable decision, but to be "fully" informed is an ideal that is seldom, if ever, realized and should not be a standard by which the FDIC should attempt to assess personal liability. AABD does not believe that it is possible for bank directors to be "fully informed", certainly not in the literal sense.

The Statement refers to a requirement to make "reasonable" decisions based on "proper deliberation." This, too has a subjective context to it – what does that really mean? The Statement does not explain what is meant by proper deliberation. We address this issue in the Recommendations section of this study.

The 1992 FDIC Statement highlights the importance of heeding the warnings of regulators and others and how not doing so can motivate the FDIC to file suit against directors.

The allegation that directors have not heeded the warnings of the banking agencies is a common one. These allegations frequently are stated in reports of examination, sometimes without much documentation or detail. Many seem to be based on the fact that the directors have not been able to successfully improve the financial condition of the institution or its loan quality or reduce concentrations. However, directors do not have total control over improving the financial condition of their institution. That depends to a great degree on the local economy. Similarly, matters such as being able to move a loan from substandard to pass, or obtaining all relevant updated financial information from a borrower who refuses to provide such information or obtaining additional collateral from an unwilling borrower are not within the power of the board to effectuate.

Failure to achieve improvement in loan quality or effectuate actions that require third party cooperation is fundamentally different from a refusal by a board of directors to do what is clearly within its power to do, such as amending a loan policy in accordance with the instructions of the examiners or adopting an ALLL methodology that the examiners instructed the bank to adopt. Our experience is that purposely flouting the authority of the banking agencies is highly unusual. Most boards of directors and management of banks want to satisfy the demands of the banking agencies particularly given the enormous power of the agencies to punish those who do not comply with their directives.

27

Notwithstanding the omissions and misstatements in this outdated Statement, directors of open banks need to take its content seriously. The FDIC has asserted on its website that it relies on the Statement to help it decide whether to sue directors of a failed bank. We will address how directors may attempt to meet the expectations of the FDIC in the Recommendations section of this Report.

RECOMMENDATIONS TO MITIGATE RISK OF PERSONAL LIABILITY

In light of the assertions made in the FDIC complaints, and based on a reading of the 1992 FDIC Statement, AABD has the following recommendations to directors of open banks:

Consider resigning.

If a director is dissatisfied with the way in which a bank is being supervised or managed and believes that this will not change, then our advice is to resign. However, resignation does not protect a director from liability for actions taken prior to the resignation.

Don't let your bank fail.

The FDIC does not sue civilly as receiver unless the bank has failed. One way for a bank director to minimize personal liability risk is to avoid a bank failure. The recommendations in this Report, if followed, will also help minimize the risk of bank failure. While bank failures in the future may not fail for the same reasons as those that failed over the past six years, it is instructive to know that most of the banks that have failed since 2009 had three characteristics in common: 1) high concentrations in CRE/ADC lending; 2) fast growth; and 3) noncore deposits and nondeposit borrowings funding that growth.

Have the knowledge necessary to meet the fiduciary duties of a bank director.

The FDIC complaints make allegations of certain director failings that would not be overcome without thorough self-education or formal training. None of the federal banking agencies require a prequalifying test or course prior to a person becoming a bank director, nor do they require any ongoing training unless imposed through an enforcement action or unless the director serves in that capacity at a national or federal savings bank with assets of $50 billion or more or at certain foreign banks. It is up to the person and the bank on whose board he or she will serve to decide what knowledge and skills are necessary for the person to serve effectively and in a manner that will minimize the risk of personal liability.

AABD offers a core course specially designed for an outside bank director, whether the director has experience serving as a bank director or not. The AABD core course covers all of the subjects that directors need to have a grasp of in order to meet the standards (we believe standards that are higher than is required by the duty of care and duty of loyalty) implicit in the FDIC complaints.

Adopt strong indemnification provisions in the articles and bylaws of both the bank and its parent company.

Depending on applicable state law, the board of directors should take action to assure that language is in the articles of incorporation or bylaws of the bank and its parent company that provides the broadest indemnification for directors as possible under state law. It is surprising how many banks do not have this language in their articles or bylaws. In addition, some banks will take the additional step of entering into indemnification agreements with their directors. If a bank fails, its indemnification of directors will have no value, but if a parent company survives, it can indemnify directors of the bank if the indemnification provisions have been properly drafted.

Adopt limitation of liability provisions in the Articles and/or By-Laws of the bank.

States permit corporations, including banks, to adopt Articles and/or By-Laws that limit the liability of directors and officers to the extent permitted by the state law. Depending on the wording, it is possible to adopt language that may effectively bar the FDIC from successfully suing directors and officers unless the FDIC can prove gross negligence or gross misconduct.

Retain a knowledgeable D&O insurance agent and confirm that the coverage for liability against regulatory actions is adequate.

Too frequently in our experience, banks have bought D&O insurance that the board thought covered them adequately against bank regulatory risk, only to find out later that the risk was not covered adequately or at all. It is essential that a bank's insurance agent be experienced and well-versed in D&O insurance policies and have access to a number of different carriers who specialize in D&O policies for banks and their directors. The FDIC has issued a Financial Institution Letter in response to an increasing number of D&O policies having carve outs and exemptions that left directors and officers unprotected in the event of a professional liability suit.[6] The Offices of the Inspectors General stated in their report on Enforcement Actions And Professional Liability Claims Against Institution-Affiliated Parties and Individuals Associated with Failed Institutions that these carve outs and exclusions were a point of concern for both the FDIC and OCC.[7] The report encouraged both agencies to ensure that directors and officers of institutions within their purview better understand their insurance policies and the potential personal liability they may face. Having an attorney knowledgeable in this coverage and policy language also can be very helpful.

Think and act defensively and with a degree with paranoia.

Once a bank fails, it can take three years and sometimes longer for the FDIC to file a suit against directors. During that period, the FDIC staff and outside counsel will pore over bank documents

---

[6] FIL-47-2013 (October 10, 2013). Found at: https://www.fdic.gov/news/news/financial/2013/fil13047.html (last visited Feb. 2, 2015). This letter also stated that bank D&O policies could not indemnify institutional affiliated parties for civil money penalties assessed against them even if the parties paid for the insurance policy themselves.
[7] Offices of the Inspector General: Federal Deposit Insurance Corporation, Board of Governors of the Federal Reserve System, Consumer Financial Protection Bureau, and Department of the Treasury, *Enforcement Actions and Professional Liability Claims Against Institution Affiliated Parties and Individuals Associated with Failed Institutions*, (July 2014). http://oig.federalreserve.gov/reports/board-actions-claims-failed-institutions-jul2014.pdf (last visited Feb. 2, 2015).

searching for information that would give them grounds to sue directors and officers. Board and board committee minutes, loan files, and other corporate documents will be scrutinized. The deliberative process of the board and its committees will be evaluated. When a board or board committee makes a decision, they should consider the possibility that another set of eyes many years from the time of the decision will be reviewing how the decision was documented but for an entirely different purpose.

Do not approve loans at the board of director or board committee level.

The FDIC complaints treat bank directors who voted in favor of approving loans at board or board committee meetings as if they are loan or credit officers. AABD recommends that directors not play that role. See Appendix IV for additional material on this issue.

If the Board or Board Committee continues to approve loans, extraordinary steps need to be taken to protect against personal liability, including thorough documentation of board and board committee decisions.

In a separate report, AABD will provide practical guidance on what steps a board or board committee can take to mitigate the risks of personal liability when approving loans. These will include having a written loan policy specifically limiting the role of the board or board committee in approving loans (that is, making it clear that they are not conducting a <u>de novo</u> review, but are relying reasonably on the work and recommendations of the lending and credit staff) and requiring loan and credit officers to make certain written representations with the presentation to the board or board committee. In addition, the loan policy should permit any exceptions to policy if approved by the board or board committee. Loan packages submitted to the board need to have sufficient information for the board to make an informed decision or where information is lacking, obtaining written confirmation that the appropriate loan or credit officer reviewed that information and was satisfied that the information was sufficient to support the approval of the loan. Every conceivable "red flag", including any variance from the loan policy and agency directives or guidance, should be identified by the loan or credit officers and documented as to how the board or board addressed the red flag, including any direction that the board or committee provided to bank management. If discussion of the loans includes discussions outside the board or board committee meetings (such as between meetings through emails and telephone calls), those discussions should be memorialized by reference to them during the official meetings and have the minutes reflect those discussions. Careful review of board and board committee minutes prior to approval by the board or board committee is also essential.

Maintain a separate, independent credit function from the lending origination function.

The credit officer must be separate from the lending officers and must report to the board, a board committee or to the CEO but only if the CEO is not a loan officer or has authority to approve loans as if he or she were a loan officer. The credit officer cannot be compensated based solely on the volume of loans booked.

Pay special attention to loan concentrations.

Before a bank decides to have loan concentrations, the board should review the benefits and risks to such concentrations, and what risk management processes need to be in place and the management resources necessary to reasonably control such risks.[8]

Document the decisions to hire and retain competent senior loan and credit officers.

Most bank failures are a result of loans going bad. The board or a board committee need not ordinarily be involved in the hiring of junior loan or credit officers and other lending staff members, but should be involved in the hiring, firing, and assessments for the senior loan and senior credit officer. If the bank is entering a new lending category or moving into a new geographic market or creating or expanding a loan concentration, the board or board committee should be involved in the process of

---

[8] *See* Federal Deposit Insurance Corporation, *Managing Commercial Real Estate Concentrations, available at* http://www.fdic.gov/regulations/examinations/supervisory/insights/ siwin07/article02_real_estate.html (last visited Jan. 12, 2015); Office of the Comptroller of the Currency, OCC Bulletin 2006-46, *Interagency Guidance on CRE Concentration Risk Management, available at* http://www.occ.treas.gov/news-issuances/bulletins/2006/bulletin-2006-46.html (last visited Jan. 12, 2015).

evaluating whether the bank has the appropriate personnel in place for such change.

Adopt, direct implementation of, and oversee a rigorous risk management system.

The FDIC complaints often make reference to deficient risk management practices. Boards and board committees should review the bank regulatory guidance on risk management to assure that they are meeting the current expectations of their banking regulators. Loan concentrations in particular require enhanced risk management systems and, in some cases, additional capital.

Assure that board reports and packages and board minutes reflect that business judgment is informed and exercised reasonably.

Decisions by boards and board committees, particularly major decisions (strategic decisions, material changes in the loan or investment portfolio, material changes in management, and approval of loans and large investments) need to be supported by the record available to the board or board committee at the time the decision was made. Many decisions involve a balancing of risk and reward, pros and cons. It's a good idea for the record to reflect that the board or board committee considered all of the factors, good and bad, in reaching its decision. Review of board and committee minutes before they are adopted or accepted should be carefully conducted to be sure that they are accurate and reflect the deliberative and prudent oversight of the board or board committee. When discussions among board members and management are held outside a board or board committee meeting that bears on the decisions being made, it is advisable that those discussions be documented during a board or board committee meeting so that the record will be clear that those discussions formed a part of the decision-making process.

Anticipate problems early through use of red flags, and take prompt corrective action once the problems are identified.

Virtually every bank, like any other business, will suffer reverses and face challenges. The banks that survive these challenges often are the ones that discover the problem early, and then take effective and timely corrective action. The identification of red flags as an early warning system is important.[9]

Establish a prudent written loan policy, an independent credit function, qualified third party loan review, and a system of checks and balances to assure effective board monitoring over the lending function.

Whether or not the board of directors or a board committee approves loans, the board is expected to establish a prudent written loan policy. This policy should be reviewed at least annually by management and the board. To help defend a board's decision to

---

[9] *See* Office of the Comptroller of the Currency, *Detecting Red Flags in Board Reports: A Guide for Directors, available at* http://www.occ.gov/publications/publications-by-type/other-publications-reports/Detecting-Red-Flags.pdf (last visited Jan. 9, 2015).

approve or amend a loan policy, it is helpful to have a qualified third party review and recommend changes in the loan policy prior to adoption. To help assure that individual loans are being made consistent with the requirements of the loan policy and underwriting standards, the board should direct management to establish an independent credit function headed by an experienced and qualified individual. A qualified third party loan review is also very helpful in providing the board with a means to monitor the loan process and loan quality. A system of checks and balances involves a series of steps and processes that the board establishes and monitors that will allow the board to monitor compliance with the loan policy and the quality of the loan portfolio; trends in the loans and loan quality, adequacy of the loan and credit personnel; and identification and resolution of risk in the loan portfolio and future lending.

Respond in writing to any and all criticisms in reports of examination, correspondence from banking agencies, and audit reports; direct that corrective action be taken; and verify that it has been taken.

Boards of directors typically rely heavily on management to respond to reports of examination. But the FDIC complaints suggest that it may be necessary for boards to take a more active role in responses. If there is disagreement with comments or conclusions in the reports of examination, it is essential that the bank respond in writing explaining why it disagrees. Where corrective action is required, the bank needs to respond in writing in a very detailed and precise way on the corrective action being taken and to request a prompt response from the bank regulator that the proposed corrective action is acceptable. The role of the board is to ask for a full briefing on the results of the report of examination, where there is disagreement, and the corrective action that is being proposed – before the response is finalized. If the board's questioning results in a disagreement with management, that disagreement needs to be worked out prior to the preparation of the final response to the banking agency. The board should also ask for updates from management as to what corrective action was taken and when it was taken, and management's corrective action should be memorialized in the minutes of the board or board committee meeting or attached to the minutes.

Take adequate steps to support the bank's efforts to comply with a formal or informal administrative action.

Boards should evaluate the adequacy of bank resources to assure that the bank will be able to comply with the terms of a formal or informal administrative action. The board role should also include careful monitoring of compliance and approval of actions required of it by the document. Use of a qualified third party such as a retired examiner to assist in the compliance effort can help the bank do a better job and also help protect the board from later criticism.

Do not pay incentive compensation that will encourage unacceptable risks.

In community banks, this issue most commonly arises in the context of paying bonuses to loan officers based on the volume of loans originated. Boards should require that incentive compensation to loan officers be also dependent on the quality of the loans being booked and the experience with such loans after booking. Some banks are beginning to use clawback provisions that will allow the bank to seek repayment of bonuses by the loan officer if the performance of the loan portfolio is unacceptable. There is bank regulatory guidance on this subject and regulations required by Dodd-Frank may be issued in the near future.[10]

Avoid insider transactions that cannot be fully justified as arms length and non-preferential.

Some boards of directors will decide that it is more prudent to decide to have no insider transactions. If insider transactions do occur, the insider whose interests are affected must disclose the conflict or apparent conflict in writing and not participate in any way in the review and approval of the transaction.

Conduct a review of policies, procedures, corporate documents and corporate governance to determine personal liability risk and how to mitigate it.

AABD now offers reviews of a bank's policies, procedures, corporate documents and corporate governance to determine what changes the board can

---

[10] Guidelines and proposed regulations can be found in OCC Bulletin 2011-13 at: http://www.occ.gov/news-issuances/bulletins/2011/bulletin-2011-13.html (last visited Feb. 2, 2015). For proposed regulations see SEC proposed rules for incentive compensation at financial institutions: www.sec.gov/news/press/2011/2011-57.htm (last visited Feb. 2, 2015).

adopt that can mitigate its members' personal liability risk.

Assume that a simple negligence standard applies to your board members even if your bank is not based in a simple negligence state.

Bank directors should assume that the FDIC will make every effort to assert a claim based on simple negligence if their bank fails. Therefore, boards of directors and board committees should conduct themselves in a manner that will avoid any allegation of simple negligence.

Periodic evaluation of the local, state, regional and national economy.

The FDIC complaints frequently assert that the board of directors of the failed bank did not take the downturn into account and continued to make CRE and ADC loans in declining markets or ones that could have been foreseen as declining. Boards of directors should reflect in their minutes discussions about the economy and how changes or anticipated changes might affect the bank's business and risks, and whether any changes in the bank's business or how it conducts business are warranted. The board of directors should be provided with sufficient information in order to reach an informed decision as to what steps, if any, should be taken in response to the changes. Once the board of directors has the information, it should be within its reasonable business judgment to decide how the bank should react, if at all, to such changes even if it turns out that the board made the wrong judgment. Changes in the economy and economic outlook could lead to changes in loan and investment underwriting standards, loan and investment type, concentrations, valuations, and other business of the Bank, including existing loans and investments.

THE FDIC COMPLAINTS

FDIC as Receiver of IndyMac Bank v. Van Dellen, et al.
Filed July 2, 2010 in the U.S. District Court for the Central District of California

The complaint was brought against four officers that were also members of loan committees but were not directors. This was one of the first complaints filed and the longest complaint with over 60 counts of negligence, waste, fraud, and breach of fiduciary duties. The FDIC sought to recover losses of over $500 million from the loss loans cited in the complaint. The bank failed with $32 billion in assets at an estimated cost to the DIF of between $4 and $8 billion.

FDIC as Receiver of Heritage Community Bank v. Saphir, et al.
Filed November 1, 2010 in the U.S. District Court for the Northern District of Illinois

The FDIC complaint alleged claims of negligence, gross negligence, and breach of fiduciary duty. The defendants were inside directors or officers, and outside directors who sat on the board loan committee that approved loss loans relevant to the complaint. The loss loans resulted in $8.5 million in losses to the bank; the FDIC sued the directors for the precise amount and over $11 million in dividends that were paid. The bank had assets of approximately $232 million when it failed.

The FDIC cited a number of issues with the bank's CRE lending. The complaint alleges the board had no experience in CRE lending and consulted no managers or outside parties with experience on how to establish a CRE lending portfolio. The FDIC claims the bank began lending in this high risk area without experience and became overly aggressive in its loan growth.

The bank had issues with underwriting CRE loans. The bank conducted poor credit analyses of potential borrowers because they did not collect sufficient information or have a complete level of secondary review. Loan officers had the opportunity to rate their own loans and often inflated the ratings. Without the second level of review, there was no internal control over this practice.

The FDIC claimed that loan concentration and underwriting issues were complicated by awarding incentive pay for originating loans without assessing the quality of the loans. The complaint claims that by allowing a single manager to receive incentive compensation and complete credit analysis and underwriting functions, the board permitted unreasonable and irresponsible incentives.

The bank's CRE loans had excessive loan to value ratios. The FDIC claimed that CRE loan amounts were dangerously close to the estimated total future value of the collateral based on an "as completed" appraisal. The bank's loan policy provided that CRE loans should not exceed 80% of the expected future value of the property. The FDIC claimed the bank routinely exceeded these limits in making CRE loans. Defendants were allegedly liable for the approving these loans without conducting a reasonable amount of diligence regarding the loan concentrations.

Regulators suggested that the bank should have monitored the CRE loans more effectively to ensure the funds dispersed were in line with the project's completion. The bank never monitored and was unaware that some projects had stalled completely. When CRE loans began to fail, the bank's tracking procedures were non-existent.

The FDIC noted improper uses of interest reserves that led to unjustified dividends and profits. Income was not received from borrowers making loan payments in cash, rather it was recognized by merely increasing the outstanding balance of the CRE loan by drawing down on interest reserves provided for in the original loan and often increased by the bank once depleted. This created false profitability for the bank and was used to justify substantial dividends to investors in the bank's holding company and generous incentive compensation programs for senior management.

FDIC claimed the defendants should have caused the bank to cease new CRE lending, aggressively work out distressed loans, increase reserves, and strengthen bank capital after the real estate market began to fail in early 2007. Instead, defendants caused and allowed the bank to make new CRE loans and to extend and renew additional advances on non-performing loans to mask their problems.

FDIC as Receiver for 1st Centennial Bank v. Appleton, et al.
Filed January 14, 2011 in the U.S. District Court for the Central District of California

The complaint was filed against officers, inside directors, and outside directors. Most of the directors also served on board loan committees and approved the specific loss loans cited by the FDIC. The claim alleged counts of negligence, gross negligence and breach of fiduciary duties. The complaint claimed simple negligence despite the gross negligence requirement under California law, established in the Castetter case in 1995. The FDIC claimed $26.8 million from the loss loans (out of a total of $163 million in losses to the DIF) and sought to recover $26.8 million from the defendants.

Bank had a high concentration of CRE/ADC loans ranging from 35-43% of total loans, whereas the bank's peers were only at 9-16% for the period from 2003 to 2008. Approximately 2/3 of the ADC/CRE loans were concentrated in single family residential tract construction loans, specifically tract housing.

The FDIC stated the bank's ADC loan to capital percentage was far too high. The bank ranked in the upper 90th percentile among peer institutions in terms of ADC loan to capital percentage, having anywhere from a 300% to over 1200% ADC loan to capital ratio prior to closing. Regulatory guidance set the limit of ADC loans to capital at just 100% and managers were on notice of this requirement. Guidance on Concentrations, 71 Fed. Reg. 74580-01, 87 (2006).

The over-concentration was a result of the bank's strategy to grow exponentially in CRE lending over five years. Most loans were made in single family tracts within a very limited geographic area. FDIC examiners warned the bank as early as March 2004 that there were problematic loan concentrations, but the bank disregarded the warnings and the proposed strategies recommended by the FDIC.

The FDIC criticized the use of brokered deposits as opposed to core deposits.

The bank had weak internal controls over lending. The FDIC specifically pointed to the following weaknesses in CRE lending: failed to mitigate losses associated with increased CRE lending, inappropriately used interest reserves, inadequately monitored concentration growth from month to month, and did not categorize CRE loans by risk for simplified review processes.

The board violated bank policies regarding prudent banking standards in the following ways: allowed loan to value ratios to exceed 75%, relied on stale financial data and failed to conduct due diligence to ensure accurate market data, did not ensure accurate collateral valuation, made loans to borrowers without any cash down payments, did not update appraisals made for various loan increases, and did not place loans on non-accrual when payment was reasonably unlikely.

The directors recklessly failed to assess market conditions by not properly determining market supply and demand via thorough due diligence. The FDIC claimed the bank should have monitored population changes, zoning requirements, rental rates and sales prices, new construction and absorption rates, and valuation trends for discount and direct capitalization rates. The FDIC asserted there was clear indication the California real estate market was declining.

The FDIC cited incompetent managers and negligent supervision issues. The bank should have ensured that compensation structures did not create conflicts of interest or perverse incentives for employees. One Vice President (Construction Lending) was in charge of too many areas (e.g., originating loans, ensuring sound underwriting, overseeing the appraisal process, and ensuring loan applications were high quality), which created a conflict of interest. The incentive compensation plan further aggravated the conflicts because that single VP could achieve over 100% of his base salary by approving a greater amount of loans. The structure encouraged strategies that disregarded loan quality in favor of loan quantity.

Outside directors were also cited for negligent oversight of managerial decisions leading to aggressive, risky lending. The complaint claims it is the responsibility of directors to ensure the careful, reasonable, prudent and non-negligent underwriting and administration of 1st Centennial's; to ensure that 1st Centennial did not engage in unsafe, unsound, unreasonable and imprudent practices; to ensure that competent management carries out the policies of the bank; must ensure that neither the compensation structure nor job descriptions create any conflicts of interests.

The complaint stated the Board "should have stopped new CRE lending by January 2007; it was a breach of the fiduciary duties . . . on the part of directors to allow 1st Centennial to be managed by officers incapable of managing the risk that the Bank's strategy . . . created."

The 2008 ROE was attached as an exhibit showing that as late as February 2007, the examiners considered the Bank as a CAMELS 2 bank, with a 1 management component rating.

FDIC as Receiver of Integrity Bank of Alpharetta, GA v. Skow, et al.
Filed January 14, 2011 in the U.S. District Court for the Northern District of Georgia

The FDIC brought counts of simple negligence, gross negligence, and breach of fiduciary duties against both inside director-officers and outside directors. Most directors were on the board loan committee that approved loans.. The simple negligence claims were dismissed by the federal judge on summary judgment; the gross negligence claims were retained for discovery. FDIC sought to recover $70 million in damages suffered from the loss loans. The bank had approximately $1.1 billion in assets when it failed. It cost the DIF an estimated $250 to $350 million.

The FDIC claimed the bank had no policies or procedures in place commensurate with the bank's extraordinary rate of growth and its risky lending strategy. The bank had one loan committee and it was only responsible for approving loans over $500,000. Only insider loans needed to be approved by the full board. The FDIC claimed this was inadequate oversight.

The FDIC claimed the bank was out of compliance with state banking regulations. The bank set its loan limit for individual borrowers to 35% of the bank's capital and surplus; Georgia only allowed a maximum loan limit for individual borrowers to 25% of capital and surplus.

Loan officers had control of both originating loans and ensuring loan quality. The FDIC claimed that this combination of responsibility created singular control over two important functions that should have been separated. Further, the combination created an even worse situation when coupled with the incentive based payments to loan officers for increasing loan volumes or generating new loans.

To attract CRE developers, the bank offered floating rate loans, interest only financing, and accepted security that contained only a small amount of equity. The collateral specifically was not sufficient to cover the loans and the loan-to-value ratio on the collateral was too high. The FDIC claimed this strategy was reckless and negligent because CRE and ADC loans were inherently risky and needed additional security to hedge against the risk.

The FDIC claimed that loan concentrations in risky loans products caused the bank to fail. ADC loan concentration dramatically increased from 2003-2007; beginning in 2005, the percentage of ADC concentration to bank capital increased from 386% to 931% without any significant increase in monitoring and reporting.

The bank failed to heed warnings from bank regulators regarding ADC loan concentration, the bank's rate of growth, and dangerously low capital levels. Regulators cited noncompliance with state banking regulations regarding loan limitations as irresponsible. The FDIC claimed the bank chose not to implement policies to remedy the problems. In fact, the bank increased lending to certain borrowers after they were warned to come into compliance. For example, one borrower was over 2.55 times the legal lending limit yet the bank granted a waiver of the limit to generate more loans.

The bank approved 15-20 loss loans to multiple parties that had issues with documentation, collateral valuation, inappropriate uses of interest reserves, and unexplainable disbursements of loan funds. These were the primary reasons the FDIC brought the action against the defendants.

FDIC as Receiver of Corn Belt Bank and Trust v. Stark, et al.
Filed March 1, 2011 in the U.S. District Court for the Central District of Illinois

FDIC brought the complaint against two inside director-officers and two outside directors who sat on loan committees. The complaint alleged negligence under state law and gross negligence under federal law against all defendants. The inside directors were also sued specifically for the loss loans for failure to administer and oversee adequate lending procedures and to protect security interests. The FDIC sought to recover $10.4 million in losses resulting in the cited loss loans. The bank failed with $260.2 million in assets and cost the DIF an estimated $79.7 million.

The FDIC claimed the board failed to adequately inform themselves of the relevant risks of CRE lending and acted recklessly in approving five high-risk CRE loans as members of the board's loan committee.
The specific loss loans cited in the complaint were improperly underwritten and extended 100 percent financing to out of state, start-up businesses; the loans were primarily secured by rapidly depreciating semi-tractors.

The two inside directors unilaterally approved and funded one loss loan after the loan committee tabled its approval. The two failed to ensure that: the loan was properly administered; the bank monitored and protected its security interests in collateral; and that the loan had adequate maintenance reserves to protect against default.

The ROEs for the bank, from 2003-2008, reflected that the bank failed to address recurring criticisms by examiners regarding imprudent lending practices, including the failure to properly underwrite, manage and administer existing credit relationships.

CRE loan concentrations equaled 307 percent of its Tier 1 Capital, and 60 percent of its loans were adversely classified. The bank reported a loss of $18.1 million primarily from imprudently made commercial loans. The FDIC noted the lending in this area was unsafe and that the board knew it was unsafe yet continued to make the loans.

Specifically, one loss loan had obvious and disclosed issues with borrower capacity. Regulators warned the board that the loan's weaknesses included the fact that they provided 100 percent financing to a start-up business located outside of the Bank's geographical area, and that the loan would be secured by the business assets, rolling stock, deposit accounts, and guarantees that were limited to only 12 percent of the debt.

Board members failed to ensure that borrowers had sufficient maintenance reserves deposited with the bank as required by the loan terms, and by failing to ensure that the bank monitored and controlled the titles to collateral.

The board was warned about the issues in multiple ROEs and MOUs beginning in 2007. The relevant MOUs sought to fix risky loan concentrations and correct violations of banking laws and regulations including capital requirements. The FDIC claimed the bank's noncompliance was gross negligence because they were on notice of the issues.

The FDIC claimed that although the bank had sound loan policies, the directors did not conduct sufficient diligence to ensure the loans they approved were in compliance with the bank's policies.

FDIC as Receiver of Washington Mutual Bank v. Killinger, et al.
Filed March 16, 2011 in the U.S. District Court for the Western District of Washington

Note: Case has been settled. The complaint was brought against three inside director-officers and two of their spouses (not directors) for simple and gross negligence, breach of fiduciary duties, and fraudulent conveyance. The FDIC sought damages to be decided at trial. The bank failed with $307 billion in assets but was sold to JP Morgan and avoided any costs to the DIF.

Defendants were experienced bankers who knew that WaMu was taking extreme risks when it focused on growing its Held for Investment (HFI) residential mortgage portfolio with multi-risk layered Option ARMs, HELOCs and subprime mortgages. Defendants also knew that strong risk analysis and management was critical to managing this type of higher risk loan portfolio. Option ARMs totaled more than $51 billion and accounted for 50% of the bank's portfolio.

The bank wanted to grow by at least 13% per year and wanted to focus on markets in Florida and California. These markets were hit the hardest by the real estate decline. The directors' attitudes were that above average creation of shareholder value requires significant risk taking. The bank was warned by managers that the growth strategy could cause capital and credit function problems.

The bank concentrated too much lending into Alt-A, subprime and ARMs. The concentrations were much higher than peer institutions and the incentives to create these loans caused the problem to worsen. Many times the bank issued loans with little or no collateral to secure the loans, with the exception of the property itself. HELOCs were also a major portfolio item and over 18% of the bank's HELOCs experienced delinquency. Subprime delinquency was over 25%.

The FDIC noted the defendants were repeatedly warned that robust risk management of Single Family Residential (SFR) lending was especially critical in light of WaMu's sales-driven culture and the Higher Risk Lending Strategy, and that risk managers would need senior management's support to be effective. As experienced bankers, defendants knew or should have known this even if they had not been warned.

The FDIC claimed the board marginalized risk in the face of multiple internal warnings from managers and outside risk consultants. Defendants knowingly suppressed discussions of SFR lending risk in meetings of the Executive Committee. They treated the Chief Enterprise Risk Officer dismissively, excluding him from important meetings, and ultimately terminated him in May 2008. Other senior risk managers also clashed with the board over their attempts to better manage the risks in WaMu's SFR lending.

The bank exhibited major infrastructure problems with technology and integration. This made it difficult for the bank to monitor results and manage lending risks in its HFI portfolio. The bank had separate platforms for its SFR lending, with largely manual rather than computerized processes and had multiple loan origination platforms that were not coordinated.

Regulatory guidance was not followed. Guidance, issued jointly by the FDIC and other federal agencies, addressed option ARMs and other nontraditional loans that allowed borrowers to defer payment of principal and interest. Regulators urged the bank to use risk management practices that the bank ultimately failed to employ, such as avoiding risk layering, having reasonable geographic and product concentration limits, maintaining tight controls, and closely monitoring lending activity.

FDIC as Receiver of Wheatland Bank v. Spangler, et al.
Filed May 5, 2011 in the U.S. District Court for the Northern District of Illinois

The complaint charged gross negligence, negligence, breach of fiduciary duties, and failure to supervise. The defendants are separated into two groups based on whether they were members of the loan committee or not. Three members of the loan committee were outside directors. Four defendants were not members of the loan committee and were outside directors but owned substantial amounts of stock in the bank. The FDIC sought to recover $22 million as a result of the loss loans. The bank failed with assets of $441.6 million and a loss to the Deposit Insurance Fund currently estimated at $136.9 million.

The FDIC cited expansive growth without the requisite experience and oversight necessary to conduct safe and sound lending. The bank had $401 million in loans, almost five times the amount promised in the business plan provided to state and federal regulators. Rapid loan growth compromised credit underwriting and credit administration, which eventually led to loan losses that depleted bank capital.

Generally, the board increased the bank's risk exposure by failing to implement prudent underwriting, risk management and credit administration practices, by failing to follow the bank's written loan policies, and by failing to properly supervise, manage, and oversee the bank's lending operations.

ADC and CRE loans represented over 1000% of bank capital in 2008 (roughly 700% in ADC loans and 300% in CRE loans). This concentration was unacceptable and against federal and state bank regulations. Peer institutions maintained concentration levels at only about 200% of bank capital. Moreover, a small group of borrowers represented 97% of bank capital, above the recommended percentage. FDIC cited these concentrations as unacceptable risk and noted the board was on notice that the concentrations should have been decreased.

Bank examiners repeatedly warned the bank about its excessive and careless growth. In multiple ROEs, the FDIC instructed the bank to decrease its concentration of ADC and CRE loans.

The FDIC suggested the bank increase its underwriting capacity and procedures to ensure complete documentation of income and credit worthiness, proper collateral valuation, improve its capital ratios, and retain qualified management.

The complaint alleged that the board should have increased its participation in the lending process, restrict total asset growth, reduce all loan concentrations, and revise and improve its lending policies. The board failed to adequately implement these suggested changes.

"The Director Defendants failed to properly supervise and oversee the Bank's lending operations. The Loss Loans were poorly underwritten and made in violation of the Bank's loan policies. The Director Defendants permitted loans to be made to favored shareholders and borrowers on terms that were preferential, abusive and harmful to the financial interests of the Bank. And they permitted the Bank to embark on an overly aggressive and risky lending strategy, which produced dangerous concentrations of CRE and ADC loans."

The board failed to supervise the lending process or loan officers. The FDIC claimed this was particularly egregious given its strong and repeated regulatory warnings to the board to get the bank's growth and underwriting procedures under control.

FDIC as Receiver of IndyMac Bank v. Perry, et al.
Filed July 6, 2011 in the U.S. District Court for the
Central District of California

The complaint was brought solely against Michael Perry, CEO and Chairman of the Board for simple negligence and breach of fiduciary duties. The FDIC claimed the loss loans accounted for over $600 million in total losses. The bank had $32 billion in assets when it failed. The FDIC estimated that losses to the DIF were between $4 and $8 billion.

Defendant allowed loan officers to issue billions of dollars in piggyback loans to borrowers for residential property. The FDIC explained the procedure as a first mortgage of up to 80% of the value of the home or collateral and a second mortgage for the remaining 20% of value. The structure left no equity in the specific homes and, thus, insufficient collateral.

Defendant acted negligently as the CEO because he allowed the bank's loans to be made with layers of substantial risk and supported a business model that encouraged risk taking. The bank did not underwrite loans purchased from other generators and had to rely upon what the other generator did or did not do as to underwriting.

76% of all the bank's loans were not properly documented and failed to undertake any proof of borrowers' income. Many of the loans had risky repayment schemes (optional adjustable rates, subprime mortgages) that, in a time of economic decline, increased the likelihood of borrower default.

Many loans were in second position (behind first mortgages) as closed-end, stand-alone second loans or stand-alone HELOCs. In 2007, the real estate market had declining values and there was a substantial risk that loans in second position would become under-secured.

The bank made a high number of loans that were generated or purchased in order to be sold into the secondary market but were held for sale for 90-180 days. The FDIC claimed that during the real estate decline, this holding period became a fundamental problem that created unnecessary risk for the bank because the secondary market was volatile. The bank needed to sell the loans quicker.

The FDIC claimed the bank wrongly emphasized production and market share over credit quality and quality underwriting. Defendant negligently elevated his desire to increase the bank's market share over prudent risk management.

Despite warnings and knowledge of serious problems in both the housing and secondary markets, defendant negligently allowed the bank to generate risky loans during 2006 and 2007 that were intended to be sold into the secondary market. However, the market became volatile and demand for the loan products decreased causing the loans to be reclassified as investment loans and ultimately written off.

The complaint cited emails that showed defendant knew the market was declining but chose to increase lending to gain market share.

FDIC as Receiver of Haven Trust Bank v. Briscoe, et al.

Filed July 14, 2011 in the U.S. District Court for the Northern District of Georgia

FDIC alleged simple and gross negligence and breach of fiduciary duty against officers, inside director-officers, and outside directors. Some of the directors were on the board loan committee while others were not. The FDIC sought to recover approximately $40 million, the precise amount caused by the loss loans. The bank's failure cost the deposit insurance fund roughly $248 million. The bank had assets of about $575 million when it failed.

The FDIC cited the following general concerns in the complaint: the bank failed to ensure adequate loan policies were in place; the bank failed to implement procedures and internal controls; the bank failed to adhere to existing loan policies, procedures and internal controls; the bank failed to ensure compliance with applicable laws and regulations; and the bank pursued a business model inconsistent with safe and sound banking practices.

The bank made multiple insider loans in violation of Regulation O and other regulations. This constituted a breach of the duty of loyalty. Directors received unsecured lines of credit and other preferential loan treatment for projects. The bank lost $7 million for one set of loans given to two directors who were attempting to form a separate business.

Collateral was a major issue cited by the FDIC. The agency alleged a number of issues with collateral including that the bank failed to inspect collateral or properly value the collateral. The FDIC claimed there were multiple items of real and personal property that were not properly perfected under state law (there was no attachment of a security interest, therefore, the collateral was subject to unsecured creditors and not subject to the secured credit protections the bank should have been granted). The FDIC noted that many appraisals were nonexistent or not properly undertaken. Various loans were under-secured as a result of the inadequate procedures.

The FDIC asserted the failure to heed regulatory warnings as a major issue facing the directors. Regulators issued multiple warnings that ADC loan concentrations and ADC capital to loan percentages were too high (around 400-600% ADC loans to capital). Capital to asset ratios were also cited as dangerously low, in the area of just 5-6% in 2008. CRE loan concentration was 58%, in violation of FDIC warnings as well as bank policy and procedures governing maximum concentrations. The FDIC claimed the defendants were on notice of these excessive concentrations.

Bank directors were cited for negligence because they were "responsible for analyzing loan applications and supporting documentation to ensure that loans were properly documented and otherwise satisfied the Bank's lending policies as well as prudent lending practices" and failed to do so adequately.

The FDIC claimed the directors were negligent because they did not satisfy their duties to select, monitor, and evaluate management; establish business strategies and policies; monitor and assess the bank's business operations; establish and monitor adherence to policies and procedures required by statute, regulation, and principles of safety and soundness; review and approve the actions of the loan committee; and make business decisions on the basis of fully informed and meaningful deliberation.

FDIC as Receiver of Michigan Heritage Bank v. Cuttle, et al.
Filed August 8, 2011 in the U.S. District Court for the Eastern District of Michigan

The complaint was brought solely against Cuttle, the bank's Senior Loan Officer, Chairman of the Senior Loan Committee ("SLC"), and Chairman of the Commercial Loan Committee. He was not a director of the bank. The complaint alleged simple and gross negligence as well as breach of fiduciary duty. The bank failed with $186 million in assets at a cost of $71.3 million to the DIF.

FDIC as Receiver of the Columbian Bank and Trust Company v. McCaffree, et al.
Filed August 9, 2011 in the U.S. District Court for the District of Kansas

The complaint brought simple negligence, gross negligence and breach of fiduciary duty claims against officer-directors and outside directors. All directors were on the Directors Loan Committee ("DLC"), the committee that approved the loss loans cited in the complaint. The FDIC sought damages from the defendants in the precise amount of the loss loans, $52 million. The bank failed with $752 million in assets and cost the DIF $60 million.

The board failed to supervise, manage and direct the business affairs of the bank to ensure compliance with the by-laws of the bank or prudent principles of banking.

The FDIC claimed the directors failed to heed warnings of bank supervisory authorities. Regulators warned the defendants that the bank's loan policies were inadequate and that the loan portfolio contained substantial inherent risks as a result of the bank's 80% concentration in commercial and CRE loans. Moreover, the regulators noted that the bank's risk levels had increased because of rapid loan growth in brokered and out-of-territory loans and the bank's loan reviews were insufficient considering the complexity of its lending.

The bank routinely made 100% financing loans to large borrowers. A number of these borrowers ultimately defaulted on their loans, which resulted in defaults that were not secured by collateral. One such borrower was a public company that disclosed its financial problems in a public 10-K; the bank continued to loan to the distressed company after the problems were disclosed. The FDIC alleged reckless and gross misconduct in lending to this borrower.

The FDIC cited the following issues with each loss loan: improper valuation of collateral; insufficient income statement verification; and inadequate monitoring to ensure completion of projects.

The bank extended credit in violation of the bank's written loan policies. The FDIC claimed the bank permitted unsafe and unsound concentrations of credit, provided financing for speculative ventures in which the borrowers invested little or no security, and extended credit to borrowers who were not creditworthy or were known to be in financial difficulty.

The FDIC alleged negligence by the board in allowing credit to be extended without adequately analyzing cash flow, debt service coverage and other critical financial information.

The board negligently relied on a credit memorandum without conducting adequate diligence. The FDIC claimed the memo, produced by a large borrower that had become insolvent, raised significant financing discrepancies with one of the bank's largest loan portfolios.

Generally, the FDIC cited the improper use of interest reserves and interest capitalization as negligent because of the discrepancies in financial statements the misuse created.

The FDIC claimed the directors failed to "review carefully each report of examination of Columbian's affairs as made by the regulatory authorities and to carry out the directions and instructions contained in such reports of examination and to establish and maintain procedures to ensure no recurrence of any deficiencies set forth therein."

FDIC as Receiver of Cooperative Bank v. Rippy, et al. Filed August 10, 2011 in the U.S. District Court for the Eastern District of North Carolina

The FDIC brought the complaint against officer-directors and outside directors for breach of fiduciary duties and gross and simple negligence. Most defendants were outside directors who sat on the loan committee responsible for approving the loss loans. The FDIC sought to recover damages of $33 million relating to the loss loans. The complaint separated claims for each loan against individual directors instead of claiming liability against all directors for all the loss loans. The bank failed with $970 million in assets at an estimated cost to the DIF of $217 million.

The bank concentrated lending in high risk ADC and CRE loans. The bank's ADC loan concentration grew from 326% of total capital in December 2005 to 469% of total capital in December 2007. In its peer group, ADC loans comprised 104% of total capital in December 2005 and 124% of total capital in December 2007.

Rather than employing methods to properly monitor and mitigate the risks associated with the highly speculative lending in which the bank was engaging, the board permitted a lax loan approval process which did not include a formal loan committee to meet, review and analyze the loans being made. The process allowed for credit renewals without adequate income verification, collateral inspection, or sufficient loan underwriting analysis.

The bank implemented a system of nine different lending limits that required only specific board member approval for all but one level. Full board approval was only required when loan's went up to the bank's legal lending limit. The FDIC claimed this was gross negligence because it failed to manage obvious risks that regulators warned were unreasonable.

The bank did not establish repayment programs on many delinquent loans and allowed the bank to become overextended, resulting in excessive credit concentrations in high risk loans, excessive loan delinquencies, excessive problem assets, violations of laws and regulations, and insufficient capital to operate the bank sufficiently.

The FDIC claimed the directors were on notice of potential issues because examiners questioned the bank's goal of reaching $1 billion in assets and raised concerns about the bank's liquidity and loan concentrations in real estate construction, development loans and beach resort properties.

The FDIC identified specific underwriting weaknesses: loans were made with little or no hard borrower equity required; analysis of the borrower's or guarantor's contingent liabilities was not performed; and stale financials and credit memoranda were relied upon to approve loans. Previously identified underwriting and administration weaknesses were not being resolved.

The compliant noted that examiners identified significant weaknesses, including liberal renewal and extension practices; inadequate analysis of the borrower's repayment capacity; inadequate borrower equity in real estate projects; over-reliance on collateral as the primary source of repayment; renewing credits without sufficient current financial information; inadequate real estate appraisals and the residential lot loan program.

FDIC as Receiver of Silverton Bank v. Bryan, et al. Filed August 22, 2011 in the U.S. District Court for the Northern District of Georgia

The FDIC brought the complaint against officers, inside and outside directors, and an insurance company for negligence, gross negligence, breaches of fiduciary duties, and waste. The bank approved loss loans in the amount of $71 million. The FDIC sued to recover the precise amount of the loss loans. The bank failed with $4.1 billion in assets at a cost of $386 million to the DIF.

"This case presents a text book example of officers and directors of a financial institution being asleep at the wheel and robotically voting for approval of transactions without exercising any business judgment in doing so."

The FDIC claimed the board was on notice of specific issues. When the OCC reviewed the bank's application to convert to a national bank charter, it gave three MRAs to the bank: resolve the CRE concentration to a more acceptable level; revisit its plan to expand and grow to ensure it makes economic sense; and develop a comprehensive capital plan to meet regulatory obligations. The bank failed to obey these directives.

A large portion of managers' compensation was based on growth and expansion. Growth goals were heavily advanced as the bank wanted to become the largest nationally-chartered banker's bank in the country. To push the bank's growth strategy, loan officers were encouraged to generate loans and were rewarded with bonuses. Loan officers received incentive compensation for creating bad loans.

The bank embarked on a course of rapid growth in the real estate construction and investment areas in markets nationwide. The bank's total assets grew from $2 billion as of December 31, 2006 to $3.2 billion as of December 31, 2008. During this time, the bank overly relied on brokered deposits, which grew to $1 billion by December 31, 2008 and then to $1.4 billion by March 31, 2009. Despite a weakening CRE market and residential real estate market volatility, the bank pursued an aggressive growth plan well past 2007 with the intent to grow out of their problems.

The bank ignored regulatory guidance. The OCC's 2006-46 Bulletin set forth that CRE lending was not to exceed 300% of a bank's capital. The bank's CRE lending ratio to capital was 1,279%.

The bank had significant weaknesses in loan underwriting, credit administration, and a complete disregard of a declining economy. The FDIC claimed the reckless manner in which loans were underwritten caused loans to be highly susceptible to negative changes in the real estate market. The board's conduct was especially egregious because they failed to correct their behavior when the economy began to decline.

Regulators found that: 1) board oversight of the lending area were inadequate; loan staffing levels were inadequate; 2) capital levels were deficient given the bank's high and increasing risk profile; 3) the quality of the loan portfolio was deficient; 4) the board and management did not effectively plan, assess, and manage portfolio concentrations; and, 5) earnings were insufficient to support continued operations and to maintain appropriate capital and ALLL levels."

The board authorized wasteful spending. The bank employed eight private pilots to carry directors and prospective clients to meetings and other locations. The bank spent nearly $62,000 annually on the shareholder meeting. In addition, the bank hosted a luxurious "Executive Management Conference" for its banking customers at the Ritz Carlton at a yearly cost of about $4 million.

FDIC as Receiver of First National Bank of Nevada v. Dorris, et al.
Filed August 23, 2011 in the U.S. District Court for the District of Arizona

Note: Case has been settled. The complaint was brought against two inside director-officers for gross and simple negligence as well as breach of fiduciary duties of care. The FDIC sought damages to be determined at trial but claimed the FDIC lost an estimated $193 million. The bank failed with $3.4 billion in assets and was purchased by Mutual of Omaha Bank. However, the estimated cost to the DIF was $862 million.

The FDIC claimed the bank concentrated its lending in Alt-A loans that were inherently risky. Despite record returns in the short-term, the strategy was reckless because the loans ended in massive losses when the real estate market softened. The terms of these loans "guaranteed" high default rates in the future and the FDIC made the directors aware of the concerns.

The bank's primary loan portfolios were dependent on perpetually increasing real estate prices, a phenomenon the FDIC claims had never happened before and that prudent directors should have known would not happen. Moreover, many loans showed no ability to be repaid but were funded and approved by the board.

FDIC cited the bank's improper underwriting policies such as not obtaining proper income verifications or allowing managers and analysts to conduct improper collateral appraisals. The bank also failed to implement risk management schemes to mitigate the risks of layered and high risk loans.

The division charged with issuing Alt-A loans did not follow the bank's own underwriting and quality assurance policies. The division recklessly issued loans to create the growth volume preferred by the board. This was cited as negligent and reckless behavior because almost 85% of the bank's lending was permitted to be concentrated in Alt-A loans.

The FDIC claimed that the board had a non-delegable duty to establish safe and sound lending policies for loan approval and underwriting. Directors delegated the duty of establishing loan approval and lending policies to lower level managers. The bank and the board also allowed investors to set lending policies that were unreasonable and not in accordance with regulatory suggestions.

Regulators consistently warned the bank and the board about its Wholesale Loan Division, the division in charge of overseeing and initiating the Alt-A loss loans. The warnings were ignored and no changes were implemented. The FDIC claimed that any activity subsequent to the warnings constituted gross negligence. The warnings came as early as August 2005. In October 2007, the bank received a CAMELS 4 rating for weakness in oversight and risky lending policies.

FDIC as Receiver for Alpha Bank & Trust v. Blackwell, et al.
Filed October 7, 2011 in the U.S. District Court for the Northern District of Georgia

The complaint was brought against inside and outside directors; most all the outside directors were on the board loan committee that approved the loss loans. The complaint alleged simple and gross negligence against all defendants. The FDIC sought to recover $23.92 million in damages, the same amount of the aggregate losses attributed to the loss loans. The bank's failure led to an estimated loss of $214.5 million to the DIF. The bank had assets of roughly $354 million at the time of failure.

The FDIC claimed the bank created a compensation structure that awarded loan origination instead of loan performance. This led to risky ADC/CRE loans and exponential ADC/CRE loan to capital growth that was not supported by internal capital growth.

The bank financed risky loans with interest reserves. The FDIC claimed this practice was discouraged because it was reckless and negligent. Using interest reserves to finance ADC/CRE loans exposed the bank to an unreasonable amount of risk if the loans became delinquent or were written off.

The bank's strategy to relentlessly grow its loan portfolio caused the bank to ignore or reject regulators' suggestions to decrease the bank's high concentration in CRE loans. Regulators and third parties warned the defendants about the excessive concentration and underwriting issues.

ADC/CRE loans accounted for 78% of the bank's entire loan portfolio; this was contrary to the bank's own lending policy, which allowed only 40% of all loans to be in ADC/CRE loans. The FDIC alleged the bank disregarded its own loan policies and created unnecessary risk in doing so.

The FDIC pointed to incomplete or inadequate lending procedures and formal policies as a reason the bank ultimately stumbled. The bank failed to create proper policies regarding loan to value ratios, proper valuation standards, and prudent underwriting standards. The bank also failed to monitor and maintain proper capital to asset ratios. This failure allowed the bank to become highly leveraged.

The FDIC took issue with the lack of documentation the bank obtained on each loan it initiated. Common problems with documentation included: non-existent appraisals, inadequate or inaccurate financial information about borrowers' sources of income or security offered, and insufficient credit investigations. The FDIC claimed the defendants were responsible for overseeing this process and hiring competent employees to follow the bank's lending policy.

The FDIC claimed the defendants were aware, or should have been aware of the deficiencies in underwriting and loan support regarding the loss loans. Despite this knowledge, the defendants approved the loss loans. The FDIC used this fact to support a gross negligence claim.

FDIC as Receiver of Mutual Bank v. Mahajan, et al. Filed October 25, 2011 in the U.S. District Court for the Northern District of Illinois

The FDIC alleged negligence, gross negligence, and breach of fiduciary duties. The defendants were inside and outside directors and officers, as well as the bank's attorney. The attorney was charged with negligence and legal malpractice. At least four defendants were close family members with the Chairman of the Board. The FDIC sought to recover $115 million from loss loans, $10.5 from unlawful dividends, and $1.09 million in wasted corporate assets. The bank failed with nearly $1.6 billion in assets. The bank's failure cost the DIF $696 million.

The FDIC cited a number of primary reasons for liability, including: the bank's reckless growth strategy focusing on ADC and CRE concentration; inadequate underwriting and credit administration practices; the bank ignored its own loan policies; the bank ignored federal lending regulations; and the bank disregarded regulators' warnings.

The FDIC made additional claims of corporate waste and improper dividend payments based on inflated company value. The directors approved $10.5 million in dividend payments that were deemed unlawful, facilitated payments for a director's wedding ($250,000) and the legal defense of a director's wife ($495,000), approved the usage of $300,000 for a director's meeting in Monte Carlo, and authorized $250,000 to pay excess amounts to contractors that were friends of directors.

ADC and CRE loan concentrations were more than three times the concentrations of peer banks. Further, concentration was focused in a small number of high volume borrowers, a concentration that exacerbates default risks. The FDIC claimed these policies were reckless and negligent.

The board failed to hire sufficient staff to support the extreme growth and concentrations into ADC and CRE lending. This resulted in many issues for the bank's documentation and loan approval procedures. The FDIC claimed many collateral appraisals were done after the loan was funded, loan guarantees were often missing from files, and loan terms were changed at closing without approval.

The FDIC alleged the bank had an extensive loan policy but failed to abide by the terms of the policy. The agency claimed this was reckless disregard and put the directors on notice that there were loan approval and documentation issues that needed to be addressed. The complaint claimed this was a failure to supervise.

The FDIC noted that regulators repeatedly warned the bank of various issues including loan concentration, improperly valued collateral, and capital requirements. One regulator warned the bank that risk management systems had not kept pace with the asset growth experienced.

The FDIC cited the bank's wasteful spending and facilitation of inappropriate payments for personal usages. This was a breach of the board's fiduciary duty of loyalty. As referenced above, the board authorized payments for individual and personal uses.

Under state law, the bank was not allowed to make any dividend payments because of its financial status as an institution not in good financial health. Yet, the bank made $10.5 million in dividend payments to its holding company, the stock of which was held almost exclusively by board members.

FDIC as Receiver of Westsound Bank v. Johnson, et al.
Filed November 18, 2011 in the U.S. District Court for
the Western District of Washington

FDIC brought the complaint against insider officer-director (Chairman and CEO) and outside directors who served on the director loan committee for breach of fiduciary duties and gross and simple negligence. The complaint made general claims against all defendants and brought specific claims regarding loss loans and insider loans against a subset of the outside directors and inside directors. The complaint sought to recover $15 million from losses relating to the loss loans. The bank failed with $334.6 million in assets at a cost of $106.4 million to the DIF.

The bank's underwriting process was problematic and lacked proper director supervision. According to the bank's loan policies, all loans over $100,000 were subject to director loan committee approval, but only one quarter of the loss loans were submitted to the director loan committee for approval.

The FDIC cited other issues including incomplete applications, LTV ratios that were dangerously high, failure to undertake appraisals of collateral, and failure to meet required debt coverage ratios. Further, the directors' responsibilities, such as ensuring sound underwriting principles and creating an adequate risk management structure were improperly delegated to low level managers.

The bank had an automated loan approval process for residential loans that could be easily manipulated by loan officers to allow any loan to be approved regardless of the safety of the loan. The FDIC claimed the bank improperly relied on the automated system. The directors were aware of this but did nothing to change the system or enforce greater oversight.

The compensation system awarded high volume production of new loans regardless of the financial soundness of the loans. Coupled with the abuse mentioned above, this created terrible incentives to cheat the system and be rewarded financially for doing so.

The bank overvalued collateral on CRE loans and approved loans with very high LTV ratios. The collateral was usually not properly appraised and was typically inflated to increase lending capacity for each project. CRE loans routinely surpassed the 85% threshold set out in the bank's lending policy. Further, ADC and CRE loan concentration were cited at dangerously high levels.

Regulatory warnings were routinely ignored by the directors and officers. A few issues that were cited were the overemphasis on asset growth, the bank's liquidity problem with capital to loan ratios, improper underwriting policies cited above, and the heavy concentration of risky ADC/CRE loans. The bank also ignored a C&D order.

The FDIC claimed the bank's lending procedures lacked appropriate checks and balances and rewarded irresponsible lending. "The defendants delegated virtually all of their responsibilities over the bank's residential construction lending function to lower level underwriters and loan officers." Specifically, the board relied on an automated system for loan approvals, failed to implement layers of review to approve and properly administer loans, and did not analyze CRE/ADC concentrations.

The bank's financial and capital deficiencies were masked by the excessive use of interest reserves. The FDIC took issue with this practice and claimed it was deceptive and manipulative.

FDIC as Receiver for Bank of Asheville v. Greenwood, et al.
Filed December 29, 2011 in the U.S. District Court for the Western District of North Carolina

The complaint was brought against one director-officer and six outside directors that either served as chairman of the board at one point or were on committees such as the board's audit committee, executive committee, and bank's loan committee. The complaint cited simple negligence, gross negligence and breach of fiduciary duties against all the defendants. The FDIC sought $6.8 million in damages from the loss loans cited in the complaint. The bank failed with $195 million in assets at a cost of $56 million to the DIF.

The FDIC claimed the defendants, as caretakers of the bank's lending function, failed to implement credit risk management policies and procedures commensurate with the inherent risks associated with a rapidly expanding and heavily concentrated loan portfolio.

The complaint alleged the underwriting process was insufficient because commercial loan borrowers were only required to submit interim financial statements annually, rather than quarterly as was required by the bank's previous underwriting policy. Moreover, the maximum LTV for commercial mortgages was increased from 75% to 80% of the lower of the purchase price or appraised value. Finally, construction loans were excepted from the written take-out requirement.

The loan committee did not have the benefit of reviewing verifying documentation such as borrower/guarantor financial statements, appraisal reviews and project feasibility studies. The practice of approving loans via email also prevented any meaningful discussion between committee members and severely limited members' abilities to conduct a complete and objective overview of the factors necessary to make informed decisions regarding the extension of credit.

The bank focused its lending growth on interest only, high risk, and CRE loans. This growth strategy was seen as particularly risky and the FDIC claimed the board was negligent in allowing the bank to embark on this policy.

To establish gross negligence, the FDIC claimed the board was put on notice and intentionally disregarded regulators' warnings over a span of approximately three years. Regulators (and auditors) identified an increasing loan concentration in CRE lending, and noted deficiencies in the monitoring and reporting of this concentration, as noted above. Together, CRE and business loans represented over 90% of all loans; CRE loans represented 470% of total risk-based capital.

The defendants failed to properly supervise the bank's mostly inexperienced and under-qualified loan officers or to ensure sound underwriting practices were enforced. Specific underwriting weaknesses included: inaccurate and inadequately supported loan presentations, inadequate analyses of borrower and guarantor contingent liabilities, inadequate verification of collateral value or feasibility of speculative projects, and no clear purpose for use of loan proceeds.

The bank used interest reserves to mask growing loan quality issues and liberal renewal policy further contributed to the masking of declines in loan quality. The policy required interest only loans to be approved and put on repayment plans after the initial time period, but the bank's loan committee routinely reauthorized interest only loans via email without credit analysis.

FDIC as Receiver for R-G Premier Bank of Puerto Rico v. Galán-Alvarez, et al.
Filed January 18, 2012 in the U.S. District Court for the District of Puerto Rico

The FDIC brought the complaint against nineteen former directors (inside and outside) and officers, seventeen of their spouses, and seventeen related conjugal partnerships, and their director and officer liability insurer. The claims were based on gross negligence and breach of fiduciary duties. There were no simple negligence claims. The FDIC sought damages of at least $257 million. The bank failed with $5.92 billion in assets at a cost to the DIF of $1.46 billion.

The FDIC claimed the board was grossly negligent because it failed to exercise due care nor any business judgment in approving obviously risky and deficiently underwritten loans. Moreover, the board negligently failed to inform themselves about, and to exercise adequate oversight over, the bank's lending function. Essentially, too much authority was delegated to loan officers.

"By ignoring the obvious risks of injury to the Bank from specific loans which they knew or should have known were extremely unlikely to be paid back, and also the equally clear risks of injury to the Bank from the Bank's inappropriate lending structure, the Directors and Officers breached their fiduciary duties of care to the Bank."

The board established a management structure that gave one director-officer complete control over the bank's credit and risk management departments.

Credit risk personnel ultimately answered to the chief loan producer, and could not effectively voice concerns about underwriting loans or borrowers' creditworthiness. Regulators repeatedly warned the board that its refusal to segregate loan production from credit risk management posed significant risk to the bank.

"Board failed to institute effective loan reviews, critically undermining its own ability to monitor the health and quality of its rapidly expanding commercial loan portfolio. Management approved many policy exceptions on a loan-by-loan basis with no mechanism to track the aggregate level or materiality." The bank's own policy prohibited more than three extensions for one loan. However, extensions were granted whenever an officer completed an extension form. The FDIC cited this practice as reckless and careless, two elements used to support gross negligence.

Regulators repeatedly warned the bank of its underwriting and credit policy deficiencies. The bank was warned that its loan concentrations and LTV ratios were dangerously high. The bank suffered decreased CAMELS ratings and had multiple C&D orders filed against them as early as 2006. However, the board did not adequately respond to regulators' complaints.

The FDIC alleged that the bank ignored its own policies for approvals and the board did not implement sufficient controls to oversee the lending function. The board did not put a proper policy in place to ensure sufficient underwriting and loan committees were reckless in their approval of the loss loans.

The directors were accused of individually approving the loss loans over the course of two years. The complaint did not separate individual loans against specific directors, however.

FDIC as Receiver of Westernbank Puerto Rico v. Garcia, et al.
Filed January 20, 2012 in the U.S. District Court for the District of Puerto Rico

The complaint brought claims of gross negligence, breach of fiduciary duty, and adverse domination. No simple negligence was claimed. The complaint listed director officers, and both inside and outside directors. Also, the complaint lists the spouses and conjugal partnerships of the defendants as required by Puerto Rico law. The FDIC sought to recover approximately $176 million resulting from the loss loans cited in the complaint. The bank failed with $11.9 billion in assets at an estimated cost of $3.31 billion to the DIF.

FDIC cited the following violations in its case summary: (1) violations of the bank's LTV ratio limits; (2) lack of required borrower equity; (3) inadequate real estate appraisals; (4) insufficient analyses of collateral or inadequate collateral; (5) insufficient borrower repayment information and repayment sources; and (6) the questionable character of the borrower or guarantor.

Additionally, the defendants repeatedly increased, extended, and/or renewed expired and deteriorating loans to enable continued funding of interest reserves.

A former director failed to disclose his substantial personal financial interest in a $12 million CRE loan before its approval, in violation of bank policies and federal regulations.

113

Specifically, the FDIC noted that the bank's CRE and construction loans lacked financial support, cash flow and debt service analyses, exceeded LTV ratio limits, and were based on faulty appraisals. Construction loans were extended, administered, and funded in violation of key loan approval terms and bank policies such as inadequate appraisals and income documentation.

The FDIC alleged certain directors were aware as early as 2005 that the bank had issues with underwriting and administering loans. One director advised the board and officers to cease lending until the administrative errors could be corrected. Yet the same director approved further loss loans. The FDIC used these facts to establish gross negligence.

The board approved, increased, renewed and/or extended the loss loans in the face of mounting examiner and auditor warnings regarding the commercial loan portfolio. In 2005, the ROE cited management's failure to correct deficiencies in loan administration and review cited in the prior year's examination. In 2006, the bank's auditors warned management of "significant deficiencies," including insufficient analysis and documentation of impaired loans.

In 2008, examiners adversely classified $1.8 billion of the bank's assets, a more than 300 percent increase from the prior year. The examiners also criticized the bank's continued funding of interest reserves on troubled projects. Despite these warnings, the board approved, increased and renewed loans in violation of the bank's approval policies, federal safety and soundness regulations, and prudent banking practices. A Form S-K in 2007 acknowledged the bank's underwriting shortcomings.

The FDIC alleged the directors were responsible for not heeding examiner and auditor warnings and correcting those deficiencies.

FDIC as Receiver for Country Bank v. Hawker, et al.
Filed January 27, 2012 in the U.S. District Court for the
Eastern District of California

The complaint alleged breach of fiduciary duties and simple negligence, but no claims of gross negligence or intent. All of the defendants were director-officers, or inside directors. The FDIC sought damages of $42 million resulting from the loss loans cited in the complaint. The bank failed with $1.7 billion in assets at an estimated cost of $135 million to the DIF.

The FDIC claimed the board members approved loans that violated the bank's internal lending policy guidelines. The loans approved contained substandard evaluation of projects, borrowers, and collateral. Loan files "lacked sensitivity analyses, failed to include sound cash flow analyses, failed to evaluate 'what if' scenarios affecting cash flows, failed to compare actual cash flows against pro forma projections, and failed to specific secondary repayment sources."

The complaint alleged imprudent growth strategy as a major cause of the bank's failure. The bank had a goal to achieve unreasonable growth and the board encouraged this goal by not implementing and overseeing proper underwriting functions. The board failed to ensure reasonable credit and financial analyses of prospective borrowers and projects.

The bank had issues with documentation requirements for the loss loans. Specific loans were approved despite insufficient guarantors required by the bank's lending policy. The bank approved ADC loans for projects that had insufficient cash flow, collateral, and inadequate financial analysis.

In 2007, the board was on notice that the real estate market was soft and was contracting in the local area. Instead of ensuring loan quality and prudent lending processes, the bank and the board continued to make high risk loans. Regulators warned the bank that its loan concentrations and underwriting failures were significant risks to the bank's health.

The bank relied on inadequate financial support as to the primary and secondary sources of repayment for many loans at a time when the bank's outstanding credit to borrowers was overextended, under collateralized and highly concentrated in high risk development loans. The complaint cited these issues as negligent and a breach of fiduciary duty. The board failed to investigate the loans before approval. Also, the board failed to take into account the overall health of the bank when approving each loan. The FDIC claimed these were essential duties that should have been completed by the board.

The FDIC alleged the board failed to use "skill and diligence in the performance of their duties, especially in connection with the bank's CRE and development lending functions, including the duty to supervise adequately those employees of the Bank under their supervision and responsibility."

FDIC as Receiver for Silver State Bank v. Johnson, et al.
Filed February 9, 2012 in the U.S. District Court for the District of Nevada

The FDIC brought the complaint against one director-officer and three officers for gross negligence and breaches of fiduciary duties; no simple negligence is alleged. Two of the officers were fired by the board prior to the complaint being filed. The FDIC sought to recover $86 million related to the loss loans cited in the complaint. The bank failed with close to $2.0 billion in assets at an estimated cost to the DIF of $450 to $550 million.

The FDIC cited the aggressive funding of high risk ADC loans with brokered deposits as particularly reckless.

The bank grew its ADC loans each year from 2006-2008, despite clear indications that the market was collapsing. Other similarly sized banks had ceased ADC loans in the region completely. The first indications of a declining real estate market and explicit warnings to the bank were made in mid-2005. One officer has admitted to knowing the local real estate market was a "house of cards."

The FDIC asserted that the bank's compensation structure exacerbated the situation because it rewarded quantity over quality loans. Risk and creditworthiness were disregarded for compensation purposes. Loan officers received a 10% bonus of all fee income earned from newly originated loans.

The growth and sources of income for the bank were extremely high compared to the bank's peers. For example, the bank ranked in the upper 95th percentile for fee and interest income, as well as asset growth rate.

In 2007, regulators told the bank that it had no formal policy regarding loan disbursements, there were too many employees with the ability to sign cashier's checks, and many construction loans were funded without using a standard voucher company that would have included site inspections.

The complaint claimed ADC loan concentration was dangerously high and remained so during 2006-2007 when the real estate market was substantially retracting. Additionally, many of the loan officers had no experience in credit analysis; they were simply charged with making new loans.

Regulators warned the bank and the board of the high concentration in ADC and speculative loans. The bank continued to increase the volume of ADC lending to reach its $2 billion in assets goal. Regulators also questioned the collateral pledged to a large number of construction and development loans. The valuation of the collateral was not adequate. Regulators also suggested the bank not use interest reserves and to adopt written policies regarding proper usage of interest reserves. ADC and CRE loans were 898% of total risk based capital, an amount strongly discouraged by regulators.

The bank's loan policies and procedures were sufficient to safely underwrite a loan and ensure credit worthiness. However, despite the bank's strong internal controls, the policies were neither followed nor enforced by managers. Loan officers and credit analysts routinely disregarded internal controls regarding income statements and creditworthiness.

FDIC as Receiver for Community Bank & Trust v. Miller, et al.
Filed February 24, 2012 in the U.S. District Court for the Northern District of Florida

The complaint was filed against two officers, only one was a director-officer. The FDIC alleged simple and gross negligence, as well as breach of fiduciary duty against both parties. Interestingly, the filing occurred in Georgia after the Integrity Bank order dismissed the FDIC's simple negligence claims. The FDIC sought to recover $11 million from the loss loans cited in the complaint. The bank failed with $1.2 billion in assets at a cost of $354 million to the DIF.

The FDIC claimed the defendants breached their fiduciary duties by approving loans that violated the bank's loan policy. Loans were approved without verified borrower financial information, adequate appraisals, and/or authorization to exceed his individual lending authority.

The inside director was negligent in failing to supervise the officers and implement corrective measures after notice in January 2006 that the officer defendant was violating the bank's loan policy and approving loans with underwriting deficiencies.

The loans at issue here were loans that were originated by the officer defendant named in the complaint. The loans were made to one customer under specific circumstances. The customer would facilitate loans for his clients in a program called the Home Funding Loan Program (HFLP) loans. "HFLP loans were high-risk, short-term bridge loans that were intended to be repaid when the investor/purchaser obtained permanent financing. The majority of these HFLP loans funded purchases of investment single family residences in the Atlanta low-end housing market, including funds for alleged repairs, renovations, and improvements."

The officer defendant approved HFLP loans without obtaining signed or completed financial statements, without appraisals, and in excess of the bank's LTV ratio limit. He also approved HFLP loans where the collateral was outside the bank's lending territory and authorized out-of-territory loans as both the primary loan officer and senior lending officer. The FDIC claimed it was negligent oversight and an unsafe lending practice to allow one officer to approve loans unilaterally without review by the board.

Although regulators were never involved in warning the bank of its underwriting violations and risky lending, the bank was made aware of the HFLP situation. One supervisor specifically wrote two memos on the subject to upper level management and the loan review committee. Despite these warnings, the bank increased lending in this area almost 400% over about one year. When a formal review was conducted, the board outlined the issues and suggested making changes to the loan policy, but ultimately decided not to do so because the officer promised to correct the situation.

The bank had a sound loan policy with effective controls. The FDIC did not take issue with the bank's policy nor the board as a whole.

FDIC as Receiver for Freedom Bank of Georgia v. Adams, et al.
Filed March 2, 2012 in the U.S. District Court for the Northern District of Georgia

The complaint was brought against directors who were members of the board loan committee for violations of state law negligence, breach of fiduciary duties, and gross negligence under federal law. One director was an inside, officer-director, while another defendant was simply a loan officer. However, three directors were named as defendants who were not members of the loan committee. The FDIC sought damages of $11 million from the loss loans cited in the complaint. The bank failed with $173 million in assets at a cost of $36.2 million to the DIF.

FDIC claimed that CRE loans were inherently risky and that fluctuations in this market were cyclical and therefore foreseeable by reasonably prudent bankers. Further, the agency claimed that ADC loans were even more risky than CRE loans.

The complaint alleged the board did not implement sound risk management, loan underwriting, or credit administration practices to accommodate for the types of loans the bank originated. The board consistently chose to delegate its loan approval duties to officers and a small group of directors by increasing the loan amounts that needed loan committee approval.

CRE loans were over 700% and ADC loans were over 400% of the bank's capital. These levels were dangerously high and regulators made the board and officers aware of these concerns in 2008.

The FDIC took issue with the bank's loan policy because it did not establish specific limits on loan concentrations, nor did it limit ADC or CRE loans in any meaningful way. The policy also did not require a global cash flow inquiry.

The above loan concentrations alone were an issue. Yet, when combined with the fact that the board did not implement any matter of protective measures, the board was grossly negligent and violated its fiduciary duties of oversight and care. The board did not establish proper loss reserves for these risky loans after accounts became delinquent.

The board approved loans with outdated financial statements and inadequate income to support repayment of the terms of the loans. The FDIC claimed the bank's own internal records regarding the loss loans made it clear that certain loans were high risk and that borrowers and their pledged capital were not sufficient to support repayment or servicing of the loans.

The FDIC claimed that in many of the loss loans, internal financial analysis determined the loans were not financially stable and were inherently risky. However, the board approved the loans to support its aggressive growth strategy.

FDIC as Receiver for Broadway Bank v. Giannoulias, et al.
Filed March 7, 2012 in the U.S. District Court for the Northern District of Illinois

The complaint was brought against seven directors; one was an officer-director, and two were officers who did not sit on the board but were members of the loan committee. All directors and officers approved the loss loans in question. The complaint alleged gross and simple negligence, as well as breaches of fiduciary duties. The FDIC sought damages of $20 million resulting from the loss loans cited in the complaint. The bank failed with $1.06 billion in assets at a cost of $391.4 million to the DIF.

The FDIC claimed the directors recklessly implemented a strategy of rapidly growing the bank's assets by approving high-risk loans without regard for appropriate underwriting and credit administration practices, the bank's written loan policies, federal lending regulations and warnings from the bank's regulators.

Starting in January 2007 and continuing through April 2009, the FDIC and other regulators made continuous efforts to curtail the risky lending the bank had pursued in the areas of ADC and CRE loans. Examiners noted weaknesses in loan administration and underwriting, including failing to obtain borrowers' current financial statements and the failure to obtain global cash flow analyses from borrowers with multiple loans.

Examiners criticized the bank's ALLL methodology for "failing to include an impairment analysis and failing to downgrade loans that were classified at previous examinations." Failure to ensure ALLL calculations overstated the bank's financial performance.

The FDIC praised the bank's internal loan policy but noted that the board and officers failed to implement or adhere to the policy in approving the loss loans. "The Loan Policy required diligent underwriting in conformity with state and federal law, close monitoring of concentrations of credit and rigorous documentation and prudent evaluation of borrower and project risk. In approving the Loss Loans, however, Defendants routinely ignored and repeatedly failed to enforce the Loan Policy's provisions. The Bank's loan approval policies also were frequently bypassed."

The bank entered at least one MOU with the FDIC to correct underwriting problems and loan concentrations in risky areas such as ADC and CRE lending. "The regulators provided a sustained and constructive critique of the Bank's operations and, through the MOU, sought a written commitment from Defendants to address the criticisms and reduce the Bank's excessive risk-taking." The FDIC claimed it was gross negligence for the board to not adhere to the MOUs.

The FDIC claimed loan concentrations were allowed to grow essentially without control, a strategy that was noted as unsafe and reckless. The bank's ADC loans were almost 800% of capital while its CRE loans were over 1100% of capital. This was more than triple the concentration of the bank's peer group in the same areas.

The complaint alleged that the bank was lending in new areas without adequate knowledge or risk management policies and expertise. "The risks associated with Broadway's portfolio were exacerbated because many of these projects were located outside of Illinois. The Bank did not have sufficient staff to monitor these out-of-state projects adequately and deferred excessively to its borrowers regarding market evaluations and risk."

FDIC as Receiver for Florida Community Bank v. Price, et al.
Filed March 13, 2012 in the U.S. District Court for the Middle District of Florida

The complaint alleged negligence under state law against both an inside director-officer and a number of outside directors who sat on the board loan committee. Further, members on the bank's audit committee were also sued because the audit committee reviewed actions by the loan committee. The agency also claimed gross negligence under federal law against all directors. The FDIC sought damages in excess of $62 million resulting from the loss loans cited in the complaint. The bank failed with approximately $870 million in total assets at a cost of $349.1 million to the DIF.

The FDIC claimed the directors ignored regulators' warnings about risky loan strategies and the practice of approving ADC and CRE loans without proper underwriting procedures such as verifying income or valuation of collateral.

The bank was operating on dangerously low capital to asset ratios and maintained little to no liquidity because of the lending strategy that focused on ADC and CRE loans. The FDIC called this strategy negligent and claimed that a reasonably prudent board member exercising sufficient diligence would not have approved the strategy or the loans.

The FDIC noted that the board failed to question management's strategies, even in spite of regulators' warnings. Moreover, the FDIC claimed the board should not have allowed Price, an executive officer and board member, to unilaterally approve loans without the board's consent or knowledge. By allowing him to do so, the board was grossly negligent. The agency claimed that the board should not have allowed any loans to be approved by Price without the board's review or approval.

LTV ratios on the loss loans were outside the bank's lending policy limitations. Despite knowing this, the board chose to approve the loss loans. The FDIC claimed the board was responsible for investigating whether these loans were compliant with the bank's policies. The failure to do so was negligent, according to the complaint.

The FDIC noted that the bank made ADC and CRE loans to consumers in markets with which the bank was unfamiliar. These out of market loans were seen as negligent and unsafe because the board was warned about the risks associated with the markets and the particular loans.

The board did not review the loan policy annually as required by the bank's policies. The board made periodic amendments but never did a thorough review of the bank's loan policy. The FDIC saw this as negligent oversight. Additionally, the board gave extensive powers to loan officers that resulted in less oversight and insufficient review of proposed loans.

The FDIC claimed the bank disregarded its commitments to the agency to make necessary changes. Despite entering a Stipulation and Consent Agreement to halt ADC and CRE lending, the bank continuously pursued a policy of risky lending and the board even adopted a formal amendment to its loan policy to originate ADC and out of market loans.

FDIC as Receiver for Omni National Bank v. Klein, et al.
Filed March 16, 2012 in the U.S. District Court for the Northern District of Georgia

The complaint was brought against three inside director-officers and multiple other officers who were not directors. No outside directors were named in the complaint. The complaint alleged negligence and gross negligence as well as corporate waste. The FDIC sought nearly $37.1 million in damages from the loss loans and wasteful expenditures. The bank failed with $986 million in total assets at a cost of $330.6 million to the DIF.

The FDIC claimed the defendants approved loans despite knowing the risks associated with the loans and violating banking regulations and the bank's internal loan policy. "These violations included, but were not limited to: (1) violations of Loan to One Borrower ("LTOB") limits through use of straw borrowers; (2) violations of Loan to Value ("LTV") ratio limits; (3) failure to obtain appraisals prior to funding and/or acceptance of stale appraisals, re-dated appraisals increased to the needed loan amount, or "drive by" appraisals; (4) lack of required borrower equity or down payment; (5) insufficient borrower credit scores or repayment ability; (6) loans to finance land flips generating seller profits of over ten percent; and (7) multiple loans on foreclosed properties to avoid or delay loss recognition."

The FDIC cited the bank's bonus policy as negligent because it awarded loan origination instead of loan soundness and quality. Year end bonuses were tied to the number of loans originated and the amount of potential fees and interest the bank could capture off the originated loans.

The bank embarked on a policy to increase real estate secured loans despite knowing in 2006-07 that the residential and commercial real estate market in the bank's lending area was declining. The bank increased risky lending by 300% over the years following 2007. "After the community development lending division (CDLD) stopped lending in December 2007, Omni increased foreclosures and rapidly accumulated OREO properties. To avoid recognizing significant losses, Omni booked many of the other real estate owned (OREO) properties at inflated "as repaired" values rather than "as is" values, in violation of federal regulations and Bank policies. Additionally, instead of selling the OREO, Klein decided to renovate many of the OREO properties for lease to low income tenants."

The board was made aware of widespread negligent and grossly negligent lending practices in the CDLD, including the following: "use of straw borrowers to circumvent LTOB limits; loans in excess of LTV ratio limits; failure to obtain required appraisals, down payments, or creditworthy borrowers; excessive "land flip" profits by which sellers bought and sold the same property at inflated values, receiving over ten percent profit in violation of Bank policy; and multiple loans to finance sales of properties in increasing amounts to avoid OREO booking and loss recognition."

In 2008, the OCC issued directives to the bank to write down a third of the OREO properties and decreased the bank's composite CAMELS ratings to a 5.

Instead of liquidating the additional OREO properties "as-is" to conserve its remaining capital, the bank expended over $12.6 million (38% of the bank's Tier 1 capital) to maintain, rehabilitate, renovate and improve additional OREO properties.

The FDIC did not take issue with the bank's lending policy, however, it noted that the officers did not comply or adhere to the standards outlined in the policy. This was cited as gross negligence.

FDIC as Receiver for Cape Fear Bank v. Coburn, et al.
Filed April 4, 2012 in the U.S. District Court for the Eastern District of North Carolina

The complaint was brought against inside director-officers and outside bank directors for breaches of fiduciary duties, negligence and gross negligence. The FDIC sought to recover $11.2 million as a result of the loss loans cited in the complaint. The bank failed with $492 million in assets at a cost of $141 million to the DIF.

The FDIC claimed the defendants' failure to establish and adhere to sound loan policies and procedures resulted in the approval of poorly underwritten and structured real estate dependent loans, including the loss loans. The agency also noted that the bank decided to continue opening new branch offices despite repeated warnings to stop expansion.

The loss loans, at the time of approval: (a) increased previously criticized concentrations, (b) violated Loan Policy and applicable laws and regulations, (c) lacked proper financial analysis or verification of the creditworthiness of the borrower and/or guarantor, and/or (d) often lacked a proper appraisal of the collateral. The inherent risks created by these improvidently granted loans were magnified when the inevitable slowdown in the real estate market began.

Rather than restricting high risk lending, working out the existing troubled loans, and preserving the bank's capital, the defendants took actions that masked the bank's problems by approving additional loss loans and renewing and making additional loan advances on non-performing loss loans. These were cited as negligent and unsafe banking practices.

The board failed to exercise independent judgment and to act in the best interest of the bank when entering, approving, and ratifying loans. The FDIC noted the board also failed to maintain or require and supervise the maintenance of adequate loan documentation. The board did not exercise due diligence and care in the supervision of the bank's officers and employees. Further, the defendants violated or permitted violation of prudent banking practices by making or permitting loans in which the sale or liquidation of collateral security was the only method by which the loan could be repaid.

The board allowed loans to be made based on grossly inadequate or inaccurate information regarding the finances of the borrower, the value of the collateral, and/or the sources of repayment. The loans were made on an under-secured basis, contrary to prudent banking practice. The FDIC noted the defendants failed to appropriately investigate borrowers' creditworthiness, representations of values contained in the borrowers' financial statements, and the actual value of collateral given as security.

The FDIC noted that the defendants approved loans in excess of 100% financing for speculative ventures and loans with excessive LTV ratios and/or deficient or incomplete appraisals.

The board failed to inform themselves and each other of the true condition of the assets and liabilities of the bank and the nature of its loan portfolio, or to review and inquire adequately into the bank's loan transactions. Further, the FDIC claimed that the board failed to establish or adhere to adequate policies and procedures prescribing the conditions and limitations under which loans could be made and the underwriting and record-keeping which should be undertaken on loans.

The FDIC claimed the defendants were grossly negligent because they failed to establish or adhere to policies responsive to the numerous warnings and criticisms by federal and state banking regulators.

FDIC as Receiver for First Bank of Beverly Hills v. Faigin, et al.
Filed April 20, 2012 in the U.S. District Court for the Central District of California

This complaint was filed against both inside and outside directors of the bank for simple and gross negligence, and breach of fiduciary duties. The inside directors were accused of simple and gross negligence. The outside directors were charged with gross negligence. All defendants were charged with breach of fiduciary duties. The FDIC sought to recover $100.6 million in damages resulting from the loss loans. Eight of the nine loss loans were participation loans with other institutions. The bank failed with $1.5 billion in assets at a cost of $394 million to the DIF.

The FDIC cited the bank's strategy and approval in making high concentrations of CRE and ADC loans allegedly without properly underwriting the loan participations. Credit analysis and valuation of collateral were two areas the FDIC specifically cited as troublesome regarding approval of the loans.

Directors did not properly inform themselves of the risks associated with making the loss loans before the directors approved the loans. The FDIC claimed the directors had an additional duty to investigate the loans before relying on the loan officers' presentation to approve the loans.

The FDIC claimed the directors had a duty to ensure loans were underwritten properly and that loans were approved in accordance with applicable regulations. The FDIC asserted that the loan approvals were continued despite warnings from regulators that the concentrations were unsafe and the approval procedures were reckless.

The FDIC noted that the board did not follow the bank's own lending policies. Loans allegedly were approved despite having insufficient income necessary to repay the loans; many loans had excessive LTV ratios that were inconsistent with the bank's lending policy.

The FDIC specifically cited that the directors relied on loan officers' due diligence and representations instead of conducting diligence themselves. California law protects directors when they reasonably rely on representations by officers regarding business decisions. The complaint stated reliance on internal credit memos was not appropriate because the memos were "facially deficient."

The FDIC cited the improper usage of interest reserves to hide losses. Interest reserves purportedly were used improperly to cover losses on loans or make loans appear to be current by shifting the reserves to show the loans were current.

The complaint alleged that the board ignored federal regulators and were therefore on notice and acting recklessly. Despite regulators' warnings, the FDIC asserts that the board did not reasonably investigate the deficiencies identified in the ROEs.

Defendants allegedly did not conduct proper reviews of the bank's loan policies to ensure the bank's loan policies were being implemented. The FDIC claimed this was negligent oversight because the board did not supervise or ensure safe and sound lending practices were being used by loan officers.

The FDIC claimed that insufficient actions were taken by the board to prevent the reoccurrence of unsafe or unsound banking practices.

FDIC as Receiver for Innovative Bank v. Hong, et al. Filed May 23, 2012 in the U.S. District Court for the Northern District of California

The complaint was brought against inside director-officers and outside directors. All defendants were sued for breach of fiduciary duties and gross negligence. The complaint separated the gross negligence claims to bring specific claims against directors. Further, the FDIC brought ordinary negligence claims against the officers only. Finally, one officer was charged with fraud. The FDIC sought to recover $7.1 million from the loss loans cited in the complaint. The bank failed with $268 million in assets at a cost of $37.8 million to the DIF.

The FDIC claimed the director defendants breached their fiduciary duties by failing to supervise the bank's SBA loan program, including not heeding regulators' and internal warnings. Moreover, the directors failed to adopt and implement appropriate SBA policies in response to regulatory criticisms and guidance that the FDIC claimed would have prevented related losses.

The complaint alleged that all defendants were grossly negligent because they failed to: 1) inform themselves about the risks of specific loss loans; 2) ensure loans were properly underwritten or properly secured with collateral; and 3) respond to regulatory and serious internal warnings regarding the risks associated with specific loans and the flawed loan approval and underwriting policies.

The director defendants were specifically charged with separate counts of gross negligence because they did not properly supervise the officers of the bank. The FDIC claimed it was the directors' duty to use ordinary diligence to assess the condition of the bank's business, and to exercise reasonable control over its officers.

Specifically, the FDIC claimed the directors failed to reasonably inform themselves about the lending activities of the officers, and failed to exercise reasonable judgment when approving loans. The failure to oversee the officers was cited as "scant care and a departure from the ordinary standard of care." The FDIC claimed the directors were grossly negligent in overseeing the officers.

The FDIC claimed the directors repeatedly ignored obvious loan policy violations causing loans to be approved that were unsoundly underwritten. This was characterized as gross negligence.

FDIC as Receiver for Community Bank of Arizona v. Jamison, et al.
Filed July 13, 2012 in the U.S. District Court for the District of Arizona

The complaint was brought against inside director officers and four outside directors. The three count charge alleges negligence by the director officers and gross negligence by all defendants. Further, a general breach of fiduciary duties charge is alleged against all defendants. The FDIC sought to recover $11 million is damages resulting from the loss loans cited in the complaint. The bank had $158.5 million in total assets and failed at an estimated cost of $25.5 million to the DIF.

The FDIC claimed that the board simply rubber stamped loan approvals without exercising any oversight or conducting independent diligence. Generally, the loss loans were claimed to have been in violation of the bank's lending policy and sound banking practices. Loans were approved with underwriting discrepancies and against applicable banking regulations.

Specifically, the FDIC claimed the directors: caused the bank to purchase loan interests that did not meet the bank's underwriting policies; failed to conduct financial analyses and appropriate collateral appraisals for specific loan purchases; did not complete borrower and guarantor financial analysis; and failed to accurately calculate or evaluate the bank's high concentration in CRE loans.

The FDIC noted that the bank's lending policy was specific and complete enough to support the board's lending approval function. However, the board did not follow specific written policies such as having loan officers conduct site inspections, completing a financial analysis of commercial real estate loans before approving the loans, and having loans be supported by independent underwriters.

The bank's high number of CRE loans were cited as an issue the board failed to address and compounded by ignoring warnings and concentration limitations. The board originated CRE loans without following proper underwriting procedures and allowed the concentration of CRE loans to exceed 60% of bank lending.

The FDIC claimed the bank ignored regulatory warnings such as published guidance and specific ROEs issued for the bank. Specifically, the bank was warned about its lower level of Tier 1 capital and the risks associated with the high concentration level of CRE loans. Despite the warnings, the bank purchased more troubled loans from other banks in 2008.

Prior to the bank's failure, the FDIC claimed it warned the bank that it had issues with its underwriting documentation. The FDIC claimed there was little oversight by the board and that no independent loan review was undertaken. The FDIC used this to say the board did not reasonably rely on staff because the board was grossly negligent in approving loans with glaring and obvious issues.

FDIC as Receiver for First Piedmont Bank v. Whitley, et al.
Filed July 13, 2012 in the U.S. District Court for the Northern District of Georgia

The complaint was brought against inside and outside directors for gross and simple negligence. Each defendant is charged under state law for ordinary negligence and under federal law for gross negligence. The FDIC sought to recover an amount to be proven at trial resulting from losses caused by improper lending to specific projects. The complaint differs from others in that it does not attach damages to the loss loans explicitly. The bank failed with $201.7 million in total assets at an estimated cost of $71.6 million to the DIF.

The FDIC claimed the directors were grossly negligent in approving ADC loans due to the failure to independently analyze the loans, properly evaluate collateral, and overlooking glaring deficiencies in the presentation of loan materials.

Despite having a strong existing loan policy, the board caused the bank to fail to follow its own LTV ratio on many of the loans it funded and violated its lending policy regarding the loan limits for a single customer. The FDIC claimed this was gross negligence.

The complaint alleged that the board did not ensure the managers or officers complied with existing underwriting policies and bank regulations for individual loans. Also, the bank did not adhere to Tier 1 capital limits.

The FDIC claimed the directors had the duty to ensure that the bank's policies were strictly followed and to take reasonably prudent steps to analyze business decisions so that the bank did not enter into unreasonable transactions. Moreover, the directors had a duty to make sure the bank did not grow at an unsafe pace in areas of lending that were unreasonably risky, and to exercise independent diligence in approving transactions and loans.

The agency alleged that ADC loans were speculative and inherently unsafe. The board should have limited its exposure to this area of lending, especially after regulators warned the bank about its underwriting issues and concentration levels. The FDIC claimed that there is a high correlation between bank failures and high concentrations in ADC loans.

Despite a strong internal policy regarding loan limitations, the board violated the policy and made changes to lending limits that were adverse to ADC loans as a ratio to Tier 1 capital. The FDIC claimed the board should not have adopted this change in policy because doing so was gross negligence.

The board did not ensure that large loans over $250,000 had the proper underwriting components such as an independent credit and collateral evaluation, a practice that was in violation of FDIC regulations.

FDIC as Receiver for Benchmark Bank v. Samuelson
Filed October 2, 2012 in the U.S. District Court for the Northern District of Illinois

The complaint was brought against inside and outside directors and officers. The directors named as defendants were all members of the Directors' Loan Committee (DLC). The complaint alleged ordinary and gross negligence against all defendants. The FDIC sought to recover at least $13.3 million in damages, the same amount of the aggregate losses attributed to the loss loans. The bank's failure led to an estimated loss of $64 million to the DIF. The bank had assets of approximately $170 million at the time of failure.

The FDIC claimed that because ADC/CRE lending is a specialized field, officers and directors should have had experience in such lending areas. The complaint claimed the defendants failed to analyze loans proposed to them and approved large loans without "sufficiently informing themselves and considering information necessary to make independent business decisions." The FDIC noted the bank lacked the necessary limits and controls to manage the large ADC/CRE loans.

Additional problems the FDIC cited with the ADC/CRE lending are were that the origination and loan administration functions were not properly segregated to allow for internal control and monitoring. Directors allegedly did not review the bank's own policies before approving loans that had multiple internal and general safety and soundness violations. Moreover, ADC concentration exceeded the bank's internal policy and regulatory guidance.

The 11 loss loans were approved despite the bank not having appropriate capital necessary to make the loans. Therefore, the bank was "forced to enter into participation agreements, under which another financial institution or institutions would buy portions of the loans in order for the bank to remain within its lending limit."

Further, the FDIC noted the bank's lending policy had material deficiencies and the defendants were warned by regulators about the issues. For example, the bank's policy listed the LTV ratio for construction loans could be 80% but regulators guidelines established a maximum 75% LTV ratio. "The policy also failed to require key underwriting data for ADC/CRE loans, such as analyses of the sales absorption period and borrower debt-service ratio."

The complaint claimed there were a number of underwriting issues with the loss loans including outdated collateral appraisals, stale financials, and insufficient credit analysis.

FDIC as Receiver for American United Bank v. Thompson
Filed October 17, 2012 in the U.S. District Court for the Northern District of Georgia

The complaint was brought against inside and outside directors and officers. The directors named as defendants were all members of the bank's Loan Committee (LC). The complaint alleged ordinary and gross negligence against all defendants. The FDIC sought to recover at least $7.3 million in damages, an amount associated with the aggregate losses attributed to the loss loans. The bank's failure led to an estimated loss of $44 million to the DIF. The bank had assets of approximately $111 million at the time of failure.

The complaint alleges, generally, that bank directors were irresponsible in taking unnecessary risks with bank loan portfolios, allowing a high concentration of ADC/CRE loans, and disregarding regulators' warnings regarding underwriting standards and lending activities. The agency also took issue with the bank buying participations without properly analyzing the risks associated with the participations and accepting outdated or inadequate underwriting standards from the other institutions.

Reckless growth strategy was a primary issue cited by the FDIC. The defendants "caused the bank to pursue an aggressive loan growth strategy focused on CRE loans, specifically ADC loans and loan participations." Thus, the defendants substantially deviated from the bank's original business plan. ADC/CRE loans accounted for 642% of the bank's Tier 1 capital. The FDIC claimed that by over-concentrating

155

"the bank's loan portfolio in CRE and ADC loans, the defendants also effectively 'turned a blind eye' to AUB's Loan Policy and prudent underwriting standards."

The complaint claimed that the defendants knew that the economy was slowing. "Despite receiving information showing a slowing of housing sales and peaking of home prices by early 2006, defendants continued to approve high risk and speculative ADC and CRE loans, including the transactions which resulted in the damages."

Regulators repeatedly warned defendants about loan concentrations and underwriting deficiencies with purchased loan participations. The defendants decided to purchase participations despite being "repeatedly warned regarding the extent of those participation loans and the lack of adequate risk management controls."

The complaint alleged that the defendants failed to hire a a qualified chief lending officer to monitor the lending process and put proper oversight measures into place to analyze ADC/CRE loans. Regulators directed the bank to hire qualified staff to address underwriting and risk issues.

The defendants repeatedly disregarded the bank's loan policy and approved loans and loan participations involving borrowers who were not creditworthy and projects that provided insufficient collateral for repayment. Moreover, the defendants repeatedly engaged in a pattern and practice of approving loans and loan purchases that: 1) violated the bank's loan policy; 2) evidenced systematic deficiencies in the credit underwriting, approval, and administration process; and 3) violated sound and prudent banking practices outlined in regulatory guidance.

FDIC as Receiver for United Security Bank v. Neese. Filed August 23, 2012 in the U.S. District Court for the Northern District of Georgia

The complaint was brought solely against the former Chief Executive Officer and bank director, Pierce Neese ("Neese"), alleging negligence and gross negligence. The FDIC seeks to recover $6.373 million in damages, which it claims was a proximate result of Neese's tortious conduct. The bank's failure on November 6, 2009 led to an estimated loss of $63 million to the DIF.

In its complaint, the FDIC makes the following allegations:

Neese functioned as a "one-man bank" and effectively controlled the loan functions of the bank even after regulators forced him to add two more people to the loan committee. As such, his strategy of rapid asset growth through ADC loans and out-of-state loan participations continued unabated despite regulatory warnings and outside factors, such as the plateau and collapse of the real estate market.

In 2002, the bank was faced with low loan demand in its home market, so the bank opened a branch office serving the Atlanta metropolitan area. The bank's growth strategy focused on CRE loans and out-of-state loan participations coincided with this geographic expansion. The FDIC cites the fact that in 2005 and 2007, the bank was more than one hundred times more concentrated in ADC loans than its peer group as cause for concern. Neese knew or should have known such concentration in CRE/ADC loans increased the bank's risk and he did not take the necessary precautions to mitigate that risk. In addition, he did not inform himself or appreciate the significance of the declining real estate market on a local and national level; he should have taken precautions to protect the bank, but instead further deepened its involvement in CRE/ ADC loans.

Neese ignored repeated warnings by regulators that the bank's loan policy was inadequate; though he did not even follow the loan policy in its deficient state. The bank's underwriting process was also deficient and Neese violated safe and sound banking practices. Sixteen loans made between 2005 and 2008 illustrate that Neese's judgment was wanting. He is not entitled to the Business Judgment Rule because of his routine failures to follow policy and his disregard for regulatory advice.

FDIC as Receiver for Ameribank v. Baldini.
Filed October 26, 2012 in U.S. District Court for the
Southern District of West Virginia

The complaint was brought against five former officers of the bank, alleging ordinary negligence, gross negligence, and breach of fiduciary duty. Three of the officers also served on the board of directors, but they are only being sued in their roles as officers. Ameribank failed on September 19, 2008 after more than one hundred years in the business, causing significant losses to the Deposit Insurance Fund; the FDIC will prove compensatory and other damages at trial.

The FDIC complaint asserts the following:

The officers contracted with a third-party mortgage broker and loan originator, Bristol, to whom they improperly delegated their duties and did not properly supervise. A bank officer has a duty to ensure that the bank operates in a safe, sound, and prudent manner; this duty cannot be delegated to a third party. The officers allowed Bristol to perform the originating, underwriting, processing, and servicing functions for the loans and Ameribank simply supplied the funds without doing its own independent analysis.

The officers wanted Ameribank to grow and a key part of the growth strategy was an increased lending portfolio. In order to keep costs down, Ameribank entered into a contract with Bristol to make rapid growth at as low costs as possible; however the arrangement was inherently risky and the officers knew or should have known that. The contract required only that the loans adhere to Bristol's lending policies and underwriting standards, which contravened Ameribank's loan policy. In addition, though the contract called for Bristol to provide certification that the loan met Bristol's underwriting standards before Ameribank would provide funds, the bank often funded the loans without a signed certification. Bristol originated low-doc CRA loans in thirteen states to individual borrowers; these loans were all under the amount requiring Board approval, so no loan was Board approved.

Though the officers did their due diligence on Bristol before entering into the contract, they did not do the due diligence required for funding risky loans. They could not contract away their obligation to follow the bank's loan policy and its underwriting standards; in addition, they had a duty to supervise Bristol once they had a contractual relationship with the third party. Because Ameribank was responsible for the funding, the officers had a duty to supervise Bristol's activities and confirm that the contract was, at least, complied with; it was not. Ameribank was specifically warned by regulators that the Bristol relationship constituted an elevated risk. Regulators stated the bank needed to hire additional loan officers, it never did; Ameribank was told to adopt new limits on assets with regard to Bristol, which it did do, but then later violated. At each turn, Ameribank failed to fulfill its obligation to put the safety and soundness of the bank first.

FDIC as Receiver for Pacific Coast Bank v. Hahn. Filed November 6, 2012 in U.S. District Court for the Central District of California

The FDIC filed a complaint against six former officers and inside directors for negligence, gross negligence and breach of fiduciary duty. The bank failed on November 13, 2009, causing a substantial loss to the DIF. The FDIC seeks to recover an amount to be proven at trial.

In its complaint, the FDIC makes the following allegations:

Pacific Coast opened its doors in 2005, but never was able to turn a profit in its four years of existence. In pursuit of some profit, defendants turned to CRE and ADC loans, known to be high-risk, but potentially very profitable. As early as 2006, regulators warned Pacific Coast that their underwriting and appraisal reviews were inadequate. Eleven high-risk, non-complying loans are offered as examples of defendants' apathy toward their loan policy, safe and sound banking practices, and basic tenets of management. Not only did defendants focus their efforts on CRE and ADC loans, but they did multiple loan participation agreements with banks outside their lending area, further exposing the bank to risk. Defendants knew or should have known about the impending economic meltdown, but they did not change their practices. Until mid-2008, they were still making loans that violated the bank's loan policy. They made loans to non-creditworthy borrowers without adequate repayment plans, they did not do independent underwriting, they did not receive acceptable financial information from borrowers or guarantors, but they still approved the applications. Defendants' behavior amounted to complete abdication of their duties to place the safety and soundness of the bank above all else.

FDIC as Receiver for Century Bank, FSB v. Florescue. Filed November 9, 2012 in U.S. District Court for the Middle District of Florida

The complaint brought against five former directors, one inside and the others outside, alleged ordinary negligence, solely against the inside directors, and gross negligence against all defendants. The Bank failure on November 13, 2009, caused an estimated loss to the DIF of $357 million; the FDIC seeks to recover compensatory and consequential damages in an amount to be proven at trial.

The FDIC complaint makes the following claims:

Director defendants, who constituted the entire bank board, had a duty to use safe and sound banking practices and to adhere to Century Bank's policies; they did neither. They followed a plan for rapid and unsustainable asset growth, concentrated in high-risk CRE and ADC loans. Ten loans, in particular, illustrate the lack of care the directors displayed in approving risky transactions.

Each of the ten loans was for over $2.5 million and therefore, according to Bank policy, required the Bank Board to approve them. The Board did not perform its due diligence and approved transactions that they knew or should have known would cause substantial losses to the bank. The ten loans offered as evidence consist of: six CRE/ADC loans, two residential real estate loans, and two loans that involved the commercial financing of speculative investment options. The Board did not adequately inform themselves of the risk involved in these loans and did not implement or adhere to proper underwriting and credit administration policies to mitigate the risks. They repeatedly ignored glaring errors in the presentations of the transactions; they did not properly assess the creditworthiness of the borrowers, including lending to people who they knew were of questionable integrity and honesty; they failed to properly evaluate the underlying real estate or collateral. In addition, they were making loans outside Century Bank's geographic territory, which meant they needed to be more careful in their evaluations, recognizing their lack of first-hand knowledge; they were not.

In December 2005, the OTS warned Century that its underwriting and loan administration policies were deficient. The Board did not follow its regulator's advice. The loans at issue were made between May 2006 and April 2009; some were made after the bank had failed to meet regulatory capital requirements and was clearly in poor financial condition. Two of the loans at issue were actually used to fund a Ponzi scheme. The directors expressed some concern about the loans to the borrower, but approved the transactions anyway. The approval was part of a quid pro quo agreement with the borrower, who had promised to invest $10 million in Century. Additionally, two of the director defendants had money invested in the Ponzi scheme.

FDIC as Receiver of Community Bank of West Georgia v. Hayden
Filed November 15, 2012 in U.S. District Court for the Northern District of Georgia

The FDIC filed a complaint alleging negligence and gross negligence of three former officers and eight former outside directors of Community Bank of West Georgia ("CBWG"). When the bank failed on June 26, 2009, it cost the DIF approximated $78.5 million. The FDIC seeks to recover $16.8 million.

In its complaint, the FDIC made the following allegations:

Defendants were responsible for operating and managing the lending function of the bank in a safe and sound manner. CBWG's business plan called for a large increase in bank assets in order to facilitate a sale within five years of opening. In pursuit of this goal, they embarked on an unsustainable rapid asset growth strategy centered on CRE and ADC loans and loan participations. These loans are high risk and need to be treated with care; defendants did not do so and they knew or should have known their behavior would cause substantial damages to the bank.

In pursuit of quick growth, defendants violated CBWG's loan policies and procedures; they also ignored repeated warnings from regulators about their lending. Prudent lending practices and the bank's loan policies required the bank to conduct its own underwriting when making a loan. Defendants relied on information from other institutions that was outdated and inadequate; they knew or should have known this increased the bank's risk of loss.

Additionally, defendants repeatedly voted to approve loans and loan participations without ensuring they were aware of all relevant information and risks. In early 2006, defendants received information from multiple sources about the declining real estate market, to which they were increasingly exposed due to the high concentration of CRE/ ADC loans. Instead of amending their plans, they continued in their strategy of high-risk lending in real estate. Twenty loans, made between May 17, 2006 and October 3, 2007, are offered to demonstrate the negligence and gross negligence of defendants.

FDIC as Receiver for Buckhead Community Bank of Atlanta v. Loudermilk
Filed November 20, 2012 in U.S. District Court for the Northern District of Georgia

The complaint against nine former officers and inside and outside directors alleges negligence and gross negligence. Buckhead's failure on December 4, 2009 caused a substantial loss to the DIF. The FDIC seeks to recover $21.8 million in damages caused directly or indirectly from the defendants' ordinary and gross negligence.

It its complaint, the FDIC asserts the following:

Defendants wanted rapid asset growth for Buckhead and chose to increase the bank's concentration in CRE and ADC loans in furtherance of that goal. Between December 2005 and June 2008, defendants approved thirteen CRE and ADC loans that exemplify their placement of asset growth over the safety and soundness of the bank. Buckhead's loan policy and prudent lending practices, generally, call for a bank to do independent underwriting before approving a loan. Defendants repeatedly approved the purchase of CRE loan participations without conducting their own independent underwriting. Defendants relied especially on the underwriting of First City Bank of Stockbridge, Georgia (*See also*: FDIC as Receiver for First National Bank of Georgia v. Lipham). First City had deficient underwriting practices and failed in March 2009. Defendants' complete disregard for Buckhead's loan policy led them to over-concentrate the bank in high-risk lending that was especially vulnerable to any decline in the real

169

estate market. Even after defendants knew or should have known such a decline was imminent, they did not change their behavior to account for the new environment.

FDIC as Receiver for First Security National Bank v. Baker
Filed December 3, 2012 in U.S. District Court for the Northern District of Georgia

When First Security failed on December 4, 2009, it caused a $43.5 million loss to the DIF. The FDIC filed suit against two former officers and five former outside directors claiming negligence and gross negligence. The FDIC seeks to recover $7.596 million.

In its complaint, the FDIC makes the following allegations:

Defendants led a rapid and unsustainable asset-growth strategy focused primarily on CRE and ADC loans. They made these loans in contravention of the bank's loan policy, prudent lending practices, and their duty to manage the bank in a safe and sound manner. Between December 2005 and February 2008, defendants approved seventeen loans that were poorly underwritten and did not comply with banking regulations or their own loan policy. Despite repeated warnings from regulators, as well as the basic tenets of finance, defendants did not diversify their portfolio but became more and more concentrated in speculative and high risk CRE and ADC loans, ultimately leading the bank to fail.

FDIC as Receiver for Rockbridge Commercial Bank v. McKinnon
Filed December 13, 2012 in U.S. District Court for the Northern District of Georgia

The FDIC filed a complaint against four former outside directors and three former officers claiming negligence, gross negligence and breach of fiduciary duty. The bank's failure on December 18, 2009 caused an estimated $107.5 million loss to the DIF. The FDIC sought to recover $27 million. On July 1, 2013, the action was stayed awaiting the 11th Circuit's decision in *FDIC v. Skow*, regarding liability for bank directors and officers.

The FDIC contended the following in its complaint:

Defendants wished to grow the bank quickly and to do so, they decided to make high-risk CRE, ADC and aviation loans, often out of territory. These loans constituted a deviation from the original business plan, but did mean quick growth. That growth proved to be unsustainable. They knew or should have known that concentrating the bank's lending in these areas significantly increased the risks. Not only did they engage in high-risk lending, but they disregarded the bank's loan policy, prudent lending practices, and effective underwriting practices. In addition, they continued approving these risky loans between 2007 and 2008, when it was clear that economic conditions were deteriorating across the country. There are sixteen loans that exemplify the lack of due care and the defendants' straying from prudent lending and underwriting practices. By mid-2009, the bank's CRE and ADC loans exceeded 7,000% of its total capital, which left the bank incredibly exposed to the real estate collapse.

FDIC as Receiver for Peoples First Community Bank v. Brudnicki
Filed December 17, 2012 in U.S. District Court for the Northern District of Florida

The FDIC filed its complaint against eight former inside and outside directors and officers, claiming negligence against the inside directors and gross negligence against all directors. The bank's failure on December 18, 2009 caused an estimated loss of $726 million to the DIF. The FDIC is seeking to recover $40 million.

On May 15, 2013, a judge granted a partial dismissal. The judge granted the motion for a more definite statement as to causation but denied the motion to strike allegations of ordinary negligence. He made note of the difference between director liability and officer liability in Florida. Directors can only be held liable if there is a conscious disregard for the best interest of the corporation, or willful misconduct and the corporation cannot indemnify them in that situation. On the other hand, officers, employees, and agents can be liable for something less than conscious disregard for the best interests of the corporation, but the corporation can indemnify them in that situation.

In its complaint, the FDIC alleges the following:

The defendants approved multiple loans, eleven offered as evidence, with numerous material deficiencies. They knew or should have known that these loans could lead to substantial losses for the bank. The eleven transactions consist of four ADC loans, one raw land transaction, and six CRE loans made between

November 2005 and August 2007. Defendants did not follow the bank's own loan policies and they violated prudent lending practices. Defendants were aware of the deteriorating real estate market and should have instituted more rigorous lending policies in light of the transactions' heightened risk; they did not. Regulators warned of the dangers of over-concentration in CRE/ADC lending and about the bank's deficient underwriting practices, but defendants continued their reckless behavior. Had they addressed concerns raised in 2005, they could have averted the bank's failure four years later.

FDIC as Receiver for Alliance Bank v. Reis
Filed December 21, 2012 in U.S District Court for the Central District of California

The FDIC filed a complaint against two former officers and four outside directors alleging negligence, gross negligence and breach of fiduciary duty. Alliance Bank failed on February 6, 2009 causing significant losses to the DIF. The FDIC seeks to recover $35 million.

The FDIC makes the following allegations in its complaint:

Defendants created and instituted a plan for rapid asset growth concentrated in high-risk CRE/ ADC loans. Between December 2005 and March 2008, they approved sixteen loans that ultimately caused Alliance a loss of $35 million. In approving these loans, defendants routinely flouted Alliance's loan policy, as well as prudent lending practices. The deficiencies of these loans were clear on the face of the Credit Memoranda delivered to defendants. In making these increasingly risky loans, and lending into a disappearing market, defendants should have instituted increased risk mitigation procedures to ensure the bank's safety and soundness. They failed to do so. Defendants knew or should have known their negligent lending practices would cause substantial losses to the bank.

Each of the defendants was a shareholder of Alliance's holding company. Instead of fulfilling their duties as directors and putting the health of the bank before everything else, they focused on balance sheet growth and their own potential profit from the bank's risk taking. Defendants were repeatedly warned of the dangers inherent in speculative CRE/ ADC lending, especially when the bank was so highly concentrated in these loans. Again, defendants did not change their practices. In June 2008, more than 70% of the bank's construction and land loans were adversely classified. By October 2008, the San Francisco Federal Reserve required the holding company to adopt a capital maintenance plan and get a capital infusion; defendants did not comply. The bank failed soon thereafter.

FDIC as Receiver for Charter Bank of New Mexico v. Wertheim
Filed January 17, 2013 in U.S. District Court for the District of New Mexico

The FDIC filed suit against nine former directors, both inside and outside, and two former officers of Charter Bank alleging negligence, gross negligence, and breach of fiduciary duty. The bank failed on January 22, 2010 and the FDIC is seeking at least $8 million in compensatory damages.

The complaint makes the following allegations:

The defendants, both directors and officers, had a duty to protect Charter Bank and ensure it only took on suitable risk; they failed in this duty. Charter Bank was based in New Mexico and its primarily lending areas were Albuquerque and Santa Fe. In late 2006, the defendants authorized the creation of a subprime lending division, Specialty Lending Group (SLG) based in Denver, CO. Defendants had no experience or presence in Colorado and they planned for SLG to lend in Florida, Texas, and California, where they believed the subprime markets were hottest. Defendants authorized and opened SLG even though they were aware of the risks of subprime lending and continued its operation even after the economic downturn made it abundantly clear subprime loans were a losing proposition.

Charter Bank committed $50 million, a full 72% of its core capital to opening and operating SLG. Defendants planned to sell the subprime loans into the secondary market, but that market was already disappearing by the time they opened SLG. Instead of acknowledging the risk as a reason for increased caution, one director called it an "opportunity" and they forged ahead with the plan, continuing until September 2008, more than a year after it was decided that SLG should be closed due to the lack of secondary market. By the time defendants finally closed SLG, Charter's subprime portfolio constituted 56.7% of its core capital and more than 70% of the SLG loans were more than 30 days past due.

Historically, Charter Bank was considered under-capitalized and over-leveraged by regulators. The bank had the second lowest core capital ratio in the OTS's Midwest Region in June 2008. OTS had previously recommended that banks with subprime programs have higher capital ratios to balance the potential risk of default; Charter Bank did not heed this warning and opened SLG while maintaining their historically low capital ratio. The defendants knew or should have known that opening SLG was an unreasonable risk to Charter Bank, but they opened it anyway. After operating SLG for less than a year, it became clear that the secondary market for subprime loans was basically non-existent and the economic downturn was imminent. Instead of closing SLG to mitigate Charter Bank's risks, defendants kept it in operation and allowed the problem to grow out of control. In addition to poor management in opening SLG, its operation fell below acceptable standards.

The subprime loan market was already suspect and the housing sector, generally, was starting to worry people. SLG's underwriting criteria fell far below the appropriate levels considering those facts and was predatory. Defendants focused not on the borrower's ability to repay but on the value of the collateral, foreseeing a multitude of foreclosures resulting in equity stripping. The OCC labeled this practice fundamentally unsafe and unsound in Advisory Letter 2003-2, dated February 21, 2003. Defendants knew or should have known that these practices were predatory; they were warned by their own Audit Committee that SLG's lending practices were cause for concern. Defendants ignored the warnings from regulators and their Audit Committee, the loans defaulted at a rapid rate – some borrowers did not even make their first payment. In November 2009, the majority of the loans SLG made were classified as substandard and Charter Bank recorded a loss of $8.1 million. Defendants committed the majority of the bank's core capital to this high-risk venture based on predatory lending practices and then continued to make subprime loans after acknowledging there was no secondary market for them and the economic environment had become even riskier than before.

FDIC as Receiver for Columbia River Bank v. Christensen
Filed January 18, 2013 in U.S. District Court for the District of Oregon

The FDIC filed a complaint against ten former inside and outside directors and officers of Columbia River Bank alleging negligence, gross negligence, and breach of fiduciary duty. Columbia River's failure on January 22, 2010 caused a loss to the DIF of $131.9 million; in this suit, the FDIC is seeking to recover $39 million.

In its complaint, the FDIC alleges the following:

Defendants began to concentrate the bank's capital in CRE and ADC lending as part of a rapid asset-growth strategy approved by defendants. Fifteen CRE/ADC loans, one agricultural line of credit, and one agricultural term loan, all approved between April 2006 and March 2008, are provided to show defendants' lax lending procedures. Defendants did not follow Columbia River's loan policy, had poor underwriting standards, did not ensure borrowers were creditworthy, and did not adhere to the prudent lending practices of the industry. They repeatedly disregarded regulators' warnings about their increased concentration in CRE/ADC loans. Defendants were aware of the deteriorating real estate market, but they did not change their practices to reflect the diminished health of the market. They knew or should have known the loans they were making would cause Columbia River to suffer substantial losses. Defendants did not implement new policies and procedures to account for the bank's increased risk, nor did they take corrective action when the riskiness of the bank's loan portfolio was pointed out to them.

FDIC as Receiver for First National Bank of Georgia v. Lipham
Filed January 25, 2013 in U.S. District Court for the Northern District of Georgia

The FDIC filed suit against eleven former officer and directors of First National Bank of Georgia for negligence, gross negligence, and breach of fiduciary duty. The bank opened for business in 1946; it failed on January 29, 2010. First National's failure caused an estimated $260 million loss to the DIF; the FDIC sought to recover $29.9 million.

The FDIC and First National settled in December 2012 for $2.1 million.

In addition to this civil suit, seven officers of First National Bank of Georgia, including three named in this suit, are subject to an ongoing criminal case. DOJ alleges these managers and officers conspired to hide the bad loans of First National as it was failing.

In its complaint, the FDIC claimed the following:

First National pursued an aggressive growth strategy primarily focused on high-risk CRE and ADC loans. Fourteen loans, made between July 2006 and February 2008, illustrate defendants' negligence and lack of due care in steering the bank. Defendants did not follow First National's loan policy or safe and sound banking principles; they did not account for the increased risk of CRE/ ADC loans. Even after they became aware of the distinctly unfriendly real estate market and received warnings from regulators, they continued to make risky and improper CRE and ADC loans. Defendants relied excessively on the inadequate underwriting done by another bank, First City Bank of Stockbridge, Georgia. (*See also*: <u>FDIC as Receiver for Buckhead Community Bank of Atlanta v. Loudermilk</u>). First City's poor lending practices caused it to fail on March 20, 2009.

FDIC as Receiver for American Marine Bank v. Townsend
Filed January 25, 2013 in U.S. District Court for the Western District of Washington

The FDIC filed a complaint against ten former directors, both inside and outside, and officers of American Marine Bank, alleging negligence, gross negligence and breach of fiduciary duty. When the bank failed on January 29, 2010, it cost the DIF $61 million. The FDIC is seeking to recover $18 million.

In its complaint, the FDIC claims the following:

From its founding in 1948 until 2004, American Marine served its local community. It had a conservative reputation and focused primarily on low-risk loans to people on Bainbridge Island and around Puget Sound; in 2004 that changed. Defendants embarked on a rapid asset growth strategy focused on out of area CRE and ADC lending. Though this change dramatically increased the bank's risk, the defendants did not take the necessary measures to mitigate the bank's exposure to the real estate market's volatility. Defendants took unreasonable risks, violated American Marine's loan policy and reasonable industry standards, especially LTV ratios, and they repeatedly ignored warnings from regulators. Eleven loans made between 2005 and 2007 consisting of two insider loans, three CRE loans, five ADC loans, and one raw land loan exemplify defendants' disregard for their duties as directors and managers of American Marine's safety and soundness. Defendants allowed inadequate underwriting and overconcentration of the bank's

187

capital in these high-risk loans, which led to the failure of a community landmark.

FDIC as Receiver for Security Savings Bank v. Jones
Filed January 31, 2013 in U.S. District Court for the District of Nevada

Security Savings Bank failed on February 27, 2009, causing a significant loss to the DIF. The FDIC filed suit against two former inside directors and one officer seeking to recover $13.1 million. The complaint alleges gross negligence and breach of fiduciary duty.

In its complaint, the FDIC alleges the following:

From 2000 to 2004, Security Savings ran a relatively unremarkable business, but in September 2004, it was acquired by Stampede Holdings, Inc. Stampede changed the bank's growth strategy to a nationwide focus on the purchase of loan participations, especially ADC loans in high-growth markets. Between 2004 and 2006, the percentage of ADC loan concentrations as a percentage of the bank's total capital grew from 17% to 306%, which constitutes an unsafe concentration. This drastic growth was not accompanied by increased risk mitigation procedures, even though defendants recognized this strategy carried greater risks for the bank. Security Savings' loan policy required independent underwriting to ensure borrowers could pay back the loans and required approval by the Loan Committee for loans over a certain amount. Defendants were members of the Loan Committee. Seven CRE and ADC loan participations are offered as evidence of defendants' complete abdication of their duties to the bank. These loans were made in violation of the loan policy and against principles of safe and sound banking. Security Savings did no independent underwriting, and defendants knew or should have known reliance on the lead bank was reckless. In addition, to make the loans appear less risky and ensure their approval, defendants withheld information and made exaggerated reports to other members of the Loan Committee and the Board. Defendants knew the loans had a high risk of loss and were under-collateralized. Not only that, they did not do adequate research about the viability of the proposed projects in light of changing market conditions.

FDIC as Receiver for Orion Bank v. Aultman
Filed January 29, 2013 in U.S. District Court for the
Middle District of Florida

The complaint filed by the FDIC against four former outside directors, who also sat Orion's Board Loan Committee ("BLC"), alleging gross negligence and breach of their fiduciary duties of care and loyalty. At the time of the bank's failure on November 13, 2009, it had $2.6 billion in assets, which caused an approximate loss of $880 million to the DIF. The FDIC is seeking to recover $53 million, which it claims represents damages incurred due to the directors' tortious conduct after August 20, 2008.

The complaint alleges the following:

The directors allowed Orion's Chief Executive Officer to pursue an irresponsible and unsustainable growth strategy focused on high concentrations of CRE/ADC loans and did not truly attempt to supervise him or the strategy. Even after the real estate market had begun to decline, the directors did not change the strategy, nor did they question the CEO's judgment. The CEO even bragged to other bank employees that the directors would never reverse his decisions, which indicates their oversight role was an empty gesture.

On August 25, 2008, the directors entered into a Written Agreement with the Federal Reserve Bank of Atlanta and the Florida Office of Financial Regulation, Orion's primary federal and state regulators, respectively. The Written Agreement effectively increased their oversight duties; it required increased scrutiny of all loans to borrowers who already had an outstanding loan and to certify that the loan was executed in compliance with Orion's loan policy. This constitutes a statement from regulators that they had been thus far derelict in their duties and should have been far more vigilant after entering into the Written Agreement; they were not.

The directors ignored proper underwriting standards, ignored Orion's loan policy, ignored the rapidly declining real estate market and the worrisome signals pointed to general economic downturn, and ignored concentration risk. The directors were generally derelict in their duty to put the safety and soundness of the bank above all else. This was exemplified by the bank's relationship with Frank Mileto, who represented himself to be a vastly wealthy Italian investor. The bank made multiple non-conforming loans to Mileto; they never verified his assets and they basically paid him for the privilege of using his name to pretend non-performing loans had been replaced by new performing loans to Mileto. Defendants never asked Mileto questions about why he was willing to purchase non-performing loans; they simply approved loan after loan, most of which the bank financed entirely, a violation of its policy. Defendants owed a duty to inform themselves about Mileto and about the multitude of loans they approved for him; they failed in that duty and were grossly negligent in not asking questions but simply rubber stamping millions of dollars in loans based solely on flawed and unverified financial information and the borrower's say-so.

FDIC as Receiver for LaJolla Bank FSB v. Colbourne
Filed February 13, 2013 in U.S. District Court for the Southern District of California

The FDIC filed a complaint against two former officers (one was also a director, but is only being sued in his capacity as an officer) and one outside director of LaJolla Bank. The complaint claims negligence, gross negligence, and breach of fiduciary duties. LaJolla Bank failed on February 19, 2010. In response to the defendants' actions, the FDIC seeks to recover $57 million.

In its complaint, the FDIC contends the following:

Defendants repeatedly ignored LaJolla's loan policy and violated prudent, safe and sound lending practices. Between March 2007 and March 2009, defendants approved seven loans that exemplify their lack of due care. The bank focused on CRE loans and defendants continued to approve them despite knowing of increasingly adverse conditions in the local real estate market. In addition, their underwriting was inadequate, especially considering the increased risk inherent in CRE loans. The defendants recommended and approved loans to borrowers who were known to be in financial difficulty, did not conduct adequate research to determine the creditworthiness of others, and approved loans with excessive LTV ratios.

One of the most compelling reasons for the focus on CRE and ADC lending was two of the defendants received a bonus based on the bank's pre-tax income. They were incentivized to make the income as high as possible and did not properly assess or plan for the increased risk; instead, they thought only about their potential profit. Defendants knew or should have known about the impending real estate collapse, but did not change their lending practices and continued lending into a failing market. Not only did they make more loans, they concealed bad loans and losses from the bank to prevent loss recognition and to maintain the loan production. Defendants were repeatedly warned by management that their lending was irresponsible and unsustainable; they ignored these warnings, as well as those from regulators.

FDIC as Receiver for Carson River Community Bank v. Jacobs
Filed February 22, 2013 in U.S. District Court for the District of Nevada

The FDIC filed suit against James Jacobs, a director, co-founder and stockholder of the bank, and member of the Senior Loan Committee ("SLC") for gross negligence and breach of fiduciary duty. The FDIC seeks to recover $3.6 million in damages in connection with three loans made by Carson River Community Bank ("Carson River" or the "Bank"), which failed on February 26, 2010, just over three years after receiving its charter.

In its complaint, the FDIC makes the following allegations:

Carson River's SLC, including Jacobs, made three irresponsible, large loans that were refinances of ADC loans extended by other banks. These loans were made soon after the Bank was chartered and constituted more than 22% of its loan portfolio in 2007 and more than 63% of its reported equity capital. Jacobs and the SLC knew or should have known there were problems with the loans prior to their approval: the credit memos provided and the minutes of the SLC meeting make it clear that they were aware the real estate market in Nevada was "softening" and that the other banks were no longer interested in these particular loans or loans of their type. Additionally, articles from the local newspaper show that people were very aware of the declining value of real estate, especially locally, which the SLC and Jacobs should have taken into account but did not.

Carson River's loan policy required appraisals to meet federal and regulatory guidelines, while their procedures technically complied, due to the declining real estate market, the Bank should have done "bulk value" appraisals instead of retail lot appraisals. The prior lender of one of the loans Jacobs and the SLC approved had threatened to foreclose on the securing collateral if the loan was not repaid in full. The SLC did not exercise the necessary due diligence in underwriting the loans: they used retail lot appraisals instead of bulk; they did not obtain a discount from the non-bank lender even though they were eligible because the debt was distressed; the comparables used were not demonstrative of the current market; and the guarantors' net worth was not reflective of their ability to pay because much of the assets in each case were either illiquid or exempt.

In addition to the poor underwriting standards, Jacobs had a conflict of interest. He was a major shareholder and director in three Oklahoma banks, two of which participated in one of the three loans at issue. When writing the loan, Jacobs included a provision that required repayment to the Oklahoma banks before Carson River; the other banks were paid in full and Carson River suffered a substantial loss on the loan. When confronted by his fellow members of the SLC, Jacobs denied knowledge of the preferential clause and Carson River did not pursue the investigation. However, according to board minutes from one of the Oklahoma banks, Jacobs absolutely knew of the preferential repayment arrangement. This subordination of Carson River's interests to those of other banks constitutes a breach of fiduciary duty.

FDIC as Receiver for InBank v. Elmore
Filed March 7, 2013 in U.S. District Court for the Northern District of Illinois

The FDIC filed a complaint against four former officers and inside and outside directors of InBank, alleging negligence, gross negligence and breach of fiduciary duties. The bank's September 4, 2009 failure caused a $66 million loss to the DIF; the FDIC seeks to recover $6.8 million.

In its complaint, the FDIC makes the following allegations:

In 2004, the bank changed its lending focus to CRE/ ADC loans in the greater Chicago area. Defendants were members of InBank's Loan Committee and approved numerous CRE and ADC loans, at least fifteen between November 2005 and October 2008, without adequate information to ensure they made an informed and prudent decision. Adding fuel to the fire, the Loan Committee was comprised almost exclusively of insiders; only one member was a non-officer and he was one of the bank's founders. This insider-dominant composition meant that the environment was not conducive to independent inquiries and judgment from the directors. One defendant was the daughter of InBank's Chairman, and fellow defendant; she was especially problematic because she ignored conditions placed on loans and the rest of the committee allowed her to do so.

In addition to a lack of information, defendants failed to abide by InBank's loan policy and either lacked or failed to demonstrate the ability to effectively understand and control the special risks associated with CRE and ADC loans. Defendants continued to loan into a deteriorating market, of which they were demonstrably aware. They also maintained the bank's concentration in CRE and ADC loans even after there was a substantial increase in past-due construction loans and increasing non-accruals. Defendants not only failed to ensure that they made loans to creditworthy borrowers or guarantors, but they did not monitor the CRE/ ADC portfolio. If they had been monitoring the portfolio as they should have, they would have seen the bank's imminent decline and possibly been able to save the InBank.

Regulators repeatedly warned InBank that their underwriting standards were not up to par, that their concentration in CRE/ ADC loans was dangerous, and that their percentage of past due and nonaccrual loans outstripped their peers. In 2007, examiners labeled the bank's condition less than satisfactory. Examiners stated that InBank's lax underwriting standards and poor supervision of the lending function were the direct causes of its deficiencies. Defendants continued to approve loans using the same criteria and process, even after receiving these warnings. Had they been exercising prudent judgment and their duty to maintain the safety and soundness of the bank, they would have changed their business plan and worked to mitigate the risks of their increased CRE/ ADC exposure.

FDIC as Receiver for New Century Bank v. Pantazelos
Filed March 26, 2013 in U.S. District Court, Northern District of Illinois

The FDIC filed suit against six former officers and directors, both inside and outside, claiming negligence, gross negligence, and breach of fiduciary duty. New Century Bank failed on April 23, 2010. The FDIC seeks to recover $33 million.

In its complaint, the FDIC claims the following:

Defendants exposed New Century to excessively high risk due to their utter disregard for the bank's loan policy and prudent, safe, and sound banking practices. Fourteen loans, both CRE and other real estate, made between April 2005 and July 2008 exemplify defendants' choice to put growth over the health of the bank. New Century had a strong loan policy, including a specific passage detailing the procedures to ensure the bank's safety in the event of a national economic downturn, like the one in 2008. However, defendants did not follow the bank's lending policies and practices. Especially worrisome was their failure to establish debt repayment programs with the borrowers, which, in addition to their lax underwriting standards, led to disaster. Furthermore, defendants expanded their lending outside the bank's normal trade area. They made CRE loans for projects in Las Vegas, NV. Defendants had no familiarity or expertise in the Las Vegas real estate market, nor did they familiarize themselves with it before lending into one of the hardest hit areas of the economic decline. Defendants knew or should have known about the softening of the market on a national scale, but they did not change their practices, which left New Century fatally exposed to the precipitous decline of the real estate market.

FDIC as Receiver for Riverside National Bank v. Smith
Filed April 15, 2013 in U.S. District Court for the Southern District of Florida

On April 16, 2010, Riverside National Bank failed causing a $491.8 million loss to the DIF. The FDIC filed a complaint against eight former inside directors and officers of the bank claiming negligence, gross negligence and breach of duties. The FDIC seeks to recover $8 million.

The FDIC makes the following allegations in its complaint:

Riverside was affiliated with three nonpublic bank holding companies; there are strict rules about accepting the stock of the bank holding company and its affiliates as collateral for loans. Defendants ignored these rules and regulations, treating affiliate stock collateral as a cash equivalent. Seven commercial loans and one consumer loan are offered to illustrate defendants' negligent lending practices. Each of the eight loans was poorly underwritten, did not conform with the bank's loan policy, and was secured largely or solely by the stock of the bank holding company's affiliates. Defendants were aware that this was risky because, on top of regulations, they were expressly told so by their independent auditor in early 2006. In response to the auditor's report and criticism from regulators, defendants adopted the 2006 amended loan policy, which specifically addressed the issue of securing loans with holding company stock. The stricter loan policy would likely have made a difference, but defendants did not follow it. The eight loans provided are rife with violations of the bank's own loan policy, as well as general industry accepted prudent, safe, and sound banking practices. On their face, the loans did not comply with Riverside's loan policy, but defendants approved them anyway, showing disregard for their duties and a complete lack of care.

FDIC as Receiver for City Bank v. Hanson
Filed April 15, 2013 in U.S. District Court for the Western District of Washington

The FDIC filed suit against one former inside director and one former officer, alleging negligence, gross negligence, and breach of fiduciary duty. City Bank failed on April 16, 2010. The FDIC seeks to recover $41 million.

In its complaint, the FDIC asserts the following:

Defendants cultivated City Bank's image into the "bank of last resort," they wanted to make loans and do deals that no other bank would touch. Obviously, this fostered a high-risk loan portfolio. Defendants made at least twenty-six loans between May 2005 and October 2008 that were in violation of City Bank's loan policy, prudent lending, and safe and sound banking practices. The bank was very heavily concentrated in risky CRE and ADC loans; it outstripped its peer group with 698% of the bank's total capital concentrated in ADC lending, as compared to 97% among its peers. Beginning in 2006, defendants received warnings about the impending collapse of the real estate market. Even so, they continued to make high-risk loans without proper underwriting or repayment plans. As early as 2007, City Bank had begun foreclosing on customers of the Construction Loan Department. Director defendant wrote multiple memoranda to the Board highlighting the inherent risks in the bank's lending practices, yet he continued to approve more loans. In addition to internal warnings, from 2005 onward, regulators stated again and again that the bank was not on safe and sound ground, that the Board needed to take measures to correct the deficiencies. The Board did not take the necessary steps to correct the imbalance and risk caused by the over-concentration in ADC loans.

FDIC as Receiver for Bank of Wyoming v. Yarrington
Filed April 23, 2013 in U.S. District Court for the District of Wyoming

The FDIC filed a complaint against seven former officers and directors of Bank of Wyoming ("BoW") alleging negligence, gross negligence and breach of fiduciary duty. Bank of Wyoming failed on July 10, 2009. The FDIC sought to recover $6.9 million.

On February 11, 2013, defendants agreed to a confession of judgment of $2.5 million and assignment of claims against their insurance.

The FDIC contends the following in its complaint:

BoW decided to pursue an aggressive growth strategy based primarily on CRE loans, most made to out-of-area borrowers. In furtherance of this goal, BoW partnered with Northland Securities and Marshall Group, Inc, both of which were based in Minneapolis. Marshall Group's affiliated bank failed in January 2010. Defendants were not familiar with Minneapolis, but they still took the lead in extending loans. Defendants completely disregarded prudent lending practices and BoW's loan policy; they routinely approved loans without even performing a basic analysis of the loan application. Regulators repeatedly warned BoW about the riskiness of their lax lending practices and advised defendants to make changes; they did not heed the warnings or advice. Defendants had a duty to ensure BoW's compliance with all relevant laws and regulations, safe and sound banking principles, and its own loan policies; they did not comply with any of them, which led the bank to failure.

FDIC as Receiver for Peninsula Bank v. Portnoy
Filed April 25, 2013 in U.S. District Court for the
Middle District of Florida

Peninsula Bank failed on June 25, 2010 causing a substantial loss to the DIF. The FDIC filed suit against four former officers, all of whom were also directors, and six former outside directors alleging negligence (only against the officer-directors), gross negligence, and breach of fiduciary duty. The FDIC seeks to recover $48 million.

In its complaint, the FDIC makes the following allegations:

Peninsula Bank had followed a traditional business plan from its inception until 2003, when defendants decided to pursue a rapid asset growth strategy based primarily on high-risk CRE and ADC loans. The bank grew rapidly, but soon it became clear that their speculative lending and deficient underwriting practices had put the bank at great risk. By 2009, the high concentration of risky CRE loans was clearly a threat to the safety and soundness of the bank.

Defendants hired independent consultants in 2005. The consultants stated unequivocally that Peninsula's lending practices and loan policy were not strict enough for the high-volume, high-risk lending in which the bank was engaging. Defendants received more and more dire warnings from the independent auditors each year until 2008, but they did nothing to mitigate the bank's risk. Not only was Peninsula's loan policy deficient, defendants did not follow it. The application documents they received for approval were deficient on their face, but defendants approved the loans anyway. This negligent behavior made Peninsula a target for land speculators throughout Florida. Thirteen loans made between July 2005 and May 2009 are offered as proof of the complete lack of due care defendants showed in approving risky CRE and ADC loans. Ultimately, these loans lost the bank $48 million directly and sped its failure.

FDIC as Receiver for Frontier Bank v. Clementz
Filed April 26, 2013 in U.S. District Court for the
Western District of Washington

The FDIC filed a complaint against six former officers and six former directors, both inside and outside, of Frontier Bank claiming negligence, gross negligence and breach of fiduciary duty. Frontier failed on April 30, 2010, causing a substantial loss to the DIF. The FDIC seeks to recover $46 million.

The FDIC makes the following allegations in its complaint:

From 2003 on, defendants pursued an aggressive growth strategy centered on CRE and ADC lending. The bank did grow rapidly and by 2009, Frontier was the largest bank in Washington and had the highest concentration of ADC loans relative to assets of any bank in the state. In achieving their goal of rapid growth, defendants violated the bank's loan policy, prudent industry lending practices, and safe and sound banking practices time after time. Eleven loans made between March 2007 and April 2008 are offered to illustrate defendants' placement of growth above the safety and health of the bank. Defendants specifically identified their niche as making these high-risk CRE and ADC loans; they also expressly recognized this niche left them vulnerable to fluctuations in the housing market. Even so, defendants kept lending into the declining real estate market, increasing the bank's potential loss exposure. They should have exercised increased care when approving new loans in the face of a sinking economy; they did not.

FDIC as Receiver for Eurobank v. Arrillaga-Torrns
Filed April 26, 2013 in U.S. District Court for the
District of Puerto Rico

Eurobank failed on April 30, 2010, causing a loss to the DIF of approximately $647 million. The FDIC filed a complaint against twenty-one defendants, including directors, their spouses and conjugal partnerships, and three insurance companies, alleging gross negligence of the directors. The complaint also calls for direct action and declaratory judgment against the insurance companies.

In its complaint, the FDIC asserts the following:

In the mid-2000s, Eurobank began to change its focus from loans to small and mid-sized businesses and their owners, executives, and employees to a portfolio dominated by CRE and ADC loans. The bank did grow rapidly, but the loans were poorly underwritten, did not conform with Eurobank's loan policy, and ultimately many borrowers were incapable of repayment.

Director defendants began this program in the midst of a recession when, instead, they should have been decreasing their exposure to high-risk loans and ensuring the preservation of Eurobank's capital. Defendants were aware of the adverse economic climate; they received a report in 2005 indicating Puerto Rico had been in a recession since 2001 and each subsequent year, it was noted that the economy was worsening. Instead of taking this into account, director defendants approved more loans, ignoring Eurobank's loan policy, bank regulations, and safe and sound banking practices.

Directors received a multitude of warnings from regulators over a period of years. In 2005, they received a warning about lax underwriting for risky loans; in 2006, the FDIC downgraded the bank management's rating; in 2007, the FDIC lowered Eurobank's CAMELS rating to 3; in 2008, they further lowered the CAMELS rating; in September 2009, director defendants agreed to a Cease and Desist Order stating they would no longer engage in certain unsafe and unsound banking practices and violations. In addition to regulatory warnings, director defendants were aware of issues with the bank. From 2004 to 2007, income decreased 80%. In 2007, an outside auditor rated their Construction Loan Department a 5, the lowest possible rating, finding multitudinous violations of laws and regulations, prudent lending practices, and Eurobank's loan policy. Director defendants continued to make non-conforming, high-risk loans for more than a year.

Twelve loans made between March 2006 and December 2008 illustrate the fact that director defendants seemingly ignored their duty to protect the bank's interests. The total loan amount was $68.15 million and the bank lost $55.47 million on these twelve.

FDIC as Receiver for Champion Bank v DiMaria
Filed April 29, 2013 in U.S. District Court for the
Eastern District of Missouri

The FDIC brought suit against ten former directors and officers of Champion Bank, alleging negligence, gross negligence, and breach of fiduciary duty. The bank's failure on April 30, 2010 cost the DIF approximately $65 million. The FDIC seeks to recover $15.56 million.

The FDIC makes the following allegations in its complaint:

Soon after its opening, Champion Bank began to pursue a high risk growth strategy based on CRE lending. Seven out-of-territory CRE loan participations and two business lines of credit made between 2006 and 2007 indicate defendants' lack of diligence in approving loans. The loan participations were in Nevada, Arizona and Idaho, far out of the bank's territory and outside of defendants' knowledge base. Not only did they lend to areas with which they were unfamiliar, defendants continued to make these high-risk real estate loans after it was clear the market was collapsing. Defendants did not do their own independent underwriting as required by Champion's loan policy and the principles of safety and soundness, but blindly trusted management's word that the borrowers could repay. Defendants repeatedly violated their duties of care and loyalty and they did not heed regulatory standards or regulator's warnings about inherent risks in CRE lending.

FDIC as Receiver for Midwest Bank and Trust Company v. Giancola
Filed April 30, 2013 in U.S. District Court for the Northern District of Illinois

The FDIC brought suit against ten former directors, both inside and outside, and eight former officers of Midwest. The FDIC alleges negligence, gross negligence, and breach of fiduciary duty and seeks to recover $128 million. The bank failed on May 14, 2010.

In its complaint, the FDIC asserts the following:

After about forty years of moderate growth, Midwest almost doubled its size in the span of two years (2001 to 2003) and planned to continue this rapid expansion. Defendants were warned by regulators that their existing policies and procedures were not adequate for a bank of their size and risk profile. In 2003, regulators found the bank had serious weaknesses in its credit management practices that left the bank vulnerable to any "slowdown in the economy," which was, of course, prescient. In 2004, regulators took formal enforcement action. In response to regulator action, the board of directors developed a new management plan, which included diversification of the bank's loan portfolio, raising capital, and double-digit loan growth. They did not achieve any objective except the loan growth, which led to further problems.

The loan portfolio became further concentrated in CRE and ADC lending and by 2007, the bank had again almost doubled in assets. The board of directors did recognize that they needed to implement new loan policies to reflect their increased risk profile and size, which they did. However, defendants did not follow the bank's loan policy. Defendants lent more than $100 million to six borrowers and their affiliated parties who were demonstrably not creditworthy; they did not do their due diligence and they did not follow the bank's loan policy or prudent lending practices. These loans resulted in damages to the bank of at least $62 million.

In addition, defendants invested in preferred stock that became classified as "other-than-temporarily-impaired" (OTTI). After an incident with Fannie Mae preferred stock, Midwest made it a policy not to acquire large blocks of thinly traded securities. Midwest also had a policy to force securities to be sold if they became classified as OTTI. Defendants defied both of these policies. They bought large blocks of GSE stock, more than $85 million in preferred stock, and then held them after they were classified OTTI. In doing so, the bank lost about $66 million that would not have occurred if defendants enforced Midwest's publicly announced policies.

FDIC as Receiver for Irwin Union Bank and Trust Company, Irwin Union Bank, FSB v. Kime
Filed May 13, 2013 in U.S. District Court for the Southern District of Indiana

The banks' failure on September 18, 2009 cost the DIF more than $1 billion. The FDIC filed suit against three former officers and one inside director of Irwin alleging negligence, gross negligence and breach of fiduciary duty. The FDIC seeks to recover $42 million.

In its complaint, the FDIC alleges the following:

Irwin Union Bank and Trust ("IUBT") and Irwin Union Bank, FSB, which was established in 2000 to move into markets IUBT was prohibited from entering, operated as alter egos. Defendants managed the banks in such a way that they basically ignored the fact that they were separate entities. Defendants were the managers of the Commercial Line of Business. They chose to follow an aggressive growth strategy, focused primarily on CRE and ADC loans. Between May 2005 and April 2009, defendants approved nineteen ADC and CRE loans in spite of clear violations of the bank's loan policy and with safe and sound banking practices. Defendants continued to make poor decisions not in the bank's best interest; they did not receive adequate financial information from the borrowers, they did not create repayment plans, and they did not account for the national economic decline.

217

FDIC as Receiver for Vantus Bank v. Backhaus
Filed May 20, 2013 in U.S. District Court for the
Northern District of Iowa

The FDIC brought a complaint against eight former officers and directors of Vantus Bank, alleging negligence, gross negligence, and breach of fiduciary duty. The FDIC seeks to recover $58 million. Vantus opened in 1923. It survived the Great Depression, but failed on September 4, 2009.

The FDIC alleges the following in its complaint:

In 2006, defendants decided to fundamentally change Vantus' investment policy. In furtherance of the goal of aggressive growth, defendants discarded prudent risk management practices. They used 120% of the bank's core capital, $65 million, to buy high-risk CDOs, which were backed by trust-preferred securities, or CDO-TruPS. In making this purchase, defendants did not perform due diligence and were either ignorant of or utterly disregarded regulatory guidance about limits on purchases of this type and the inherent risk in these instruments. Defendants made the purchases between October 2006 and March 2007, which fell between OTS examinations. In December 2001, OTS issued Thrift Bulletin 73a, which stated limits on purchases of these instruments. In TB 73a, OTS limited purchases of these instruments to no more than 15% of the bank's capital, but Vantus' purchases were eight times that limit. In addition, OTS placed a $12.5 million limit on purchases from a single issuer; at least two of Vantus' purchases exceeded this limit.

In making these purchases, director defendants relied on the representations of risk made by officer defendants. Directors should have known that the officers did not perform due diligence. The officers had no knowledge of TB 73a and did not research CDO-TruPS before recommending the majority of the bank's core capital be placed in these risky and opaque investment instruments. In fact, they relied almost solely on the representations made by the investment bank and broker-dealers selling them the CDo-TruPS, even though they knew or should have known the investment bank had a pecuniary interest in selling them CDO-TruPS. After OTS became aware of the purchases, it directed Vantus to sell two of the CDO-TruPS and not to buy any more. Though defendants agreed to the do as OTS instructed them, they did sell any of the CDO-TruPS.

FDIC as Receiver for Sun West Bank v. Delaney. Filed May 24, 2013 in U.S. District Court for the District of Nevada

The complaint was brought against nine inside and outside directors and officers, three of whom served on the Management Loan Committee ("MLC"). The FDIC alleges gross negligence and breaches of fiduciary duty, which caused the bank to fail on May 28, 2010. The FDIC is seeking to recover $8 million in damages, which it claims represents lost profits, lost operating capital and lost investment opportunities.

The defendants' goal was to grow the bank to over $1 billion in assets in ten years, which they pursued to the detriment of the overall health of the bank. In their attempts to reach $1 billion, they violated prudent lending practices, did not follow the bank's own loan policy, and ignored regulatory advice. They aggressively extended credit in ever more risky and speculative CRE and ADC lending, over-concentrating the bank in that area. The FDIC notes that there are special risks involved with CRE/ ADC lending; both the FDIC on its own and the FDIC, OCC and FRB, jointly, have issued guidance to financial institutions on the risks and how to lend responsibly in that specialized field.

In addition to general guidance, the FDIC maintains that the defendants were repeatedly warned by regulators, outside counsel, and by the bank's own Credit Administrative Officer ("CAO") that the bank was becoming over-concentrated in risky loans and that they were not following sound lending practices. In 2007, FDIC examiners noted that while the bank was sound, CRE-secured loans amounted to 717% of Tier 1 capital, which was a dramatic increase from the previous year and could be cause for concern. The bank's counsel authored a monthly banking periodical, which repeatedly noted the downward trend of the real estate market and mentioned that some financial institutions were running into trouble due to CRE loans. The CAO continually tried to convince the defendants that they should heed the regulators' and outside counsel's warnings and change their lending practices. He was ignored and fired. The bank did not change its practices.

The bank did have a loan policy, which, provided for prudent, safe and sound underwriting but which was not followed by the defendants. The FDIC alleges the defendants engaged in the following, in violation of policy: speculative lending, loans to non-creditworthy borrowers, loans to non-credit-worthy LLCs, excessive LTV ratios, overreliance on interest reserves, loans to borrowers with improper equity investments, inadequate financial analysis, and improper renewals or extensions. The complaint offers six loans as illustrations for these failures.

FDIC as Receiver for TierOne Bank v. Lundstrom
Filed May 31, 2013 in U.S. District Court for the
District of Nebraska

The FDIC filed suit against five former inside and outside directors and three former officers of TierOne Bank, alleging gross negligence and breach of fiduciary duty. The bank failed on June 4, 2010. The FDIC seeks to recover $40 million.

The FDIC asserts the following in its complaint:

TierOne Bank was founded in 1907. It survived the Great Depression and the S&L Crisis, but in 2004, defendants decided to pursue an aggressive growth strategy hoping to quickly grow the bank's assets. They focused on CRE and ADC lending, but did not take proper steps to manage the increased risk. Defendants wanted to create "Turbo Assets," which are high risk and have higher interest rates than traditional mortgage loans, and wanted to focus on Las Vegas, NV, where they had no familiarity or experience. TierOne had, for almost a century, made primarily home and traditional business loans in its community and had more than $2 billion in assets. Defendants abandoned this model. By 2006, they had $3.4 billion in assets.

TierOne changed its compensation model to award quantity over quality. Defendants were awarded based on loan origination, not loan quality and were not held accountable for loan performance. Thus, officer defendants began to recommend more and more loans that violated the bank's loan policy and prudent lending practices and director defendants approved them. Eight ADC loans made between April

2006 and September 2008 are illustrative of the placement of the potential for profit over long-term longevity and health of the bank. Not only did defendants approve the loans originally, but they modified and extended the loan terms, which gave the delinquent borrowers more time and meant that TierOne's improper lending practices took longer to come to light. Part of the problem was that the bank had no loan committee and the directors who had authority to approve loans simply did so over the phone after limited discussion. Additionally, Las Vegas was a particularly inflated and volatile market, with which, again, defendants were unfamiliar. Defendants continued lending into the Vegas real estate market even after it was clear it was collapsing, making TierOne even more vulnerable.

FDIC as Receiver for Sun American Bank v. Castro
Filed June 10, 2013 in U.S. District Court for the Southern District of Florida

The FDIC filed suit against five former directors, both inside and outside, and two former officers of Sun American Bank, alleging negligence against the inside directors and officers and gross negligence against all defendants. When the bank failed on March 5, 2010, it cost the DIF approximately $158.7 million. The FDIC seeks to recover $12.617 million.

In its complaint, the FDIC claims the following:

In 2005, defendants devised a new strategy to quadruple the bank's assets in four years: increased lending and acquiring assets of other financial institutions. Defendants dove headlong into the plan; even when it became clear that the economy was not cooperating with increased growth, they continued to lend into the sagging real estate market. Between November 2005 and June 2008, defendants approved seven transactions, five CRE loans, one ADC loan, and one commercial transaction, secured by bank stock, extending credit to a bank holding company, none of which complied with the bank's loan policy or safe and sound banking practices. In approving these loans, defendants demonstrated complete disregard for their duties to the bank; they knew or should have known these loans would cause damage to Sun American.

From 2006, regulators criticized defendants about their poor risk management and poor underwriting. Because defendants still had the goal of reaching $1 billion in assets, they did not alter their non-conforming behavior. Defendant's practices did not change to be commensurate with the increased risk, both of the higher-risk loans and the higher-risk environment into which they were now lending. Even after suffering consistent losses over a period of years, defendants did not heed regulators warnings or reevaluate their practices.

FDIC as Receiver for Advanta Bank Corp. v. Alter.
Filed June 17, 2013 in U.S. District Court for the
Eastern District of Pennsylvania

The FDIC brought a complaint against two former officers and inside directors, sued in their capacity as officers with control over the Bank's management and operations, alleging gross negligence and breach of fiduciary duty. The failure of Advanta Bank Corp on March 19, 2010 marked the only major credit card issuer to go into insolvency during the Financial Crisis. The FDIC seeks to recover $219 million in damages due to the actions taken by the officers.

In its complaint, the FDIC asserts the following:

Advanta embarked on an aggressive re-pricing campaign, increasing its credit card interest rates to unprecedented levels, which drove away its customer base. The motive for doing so was to maintain the Bank's dividends to Advanta's holding company and prop up the holding company's stock price, both of which were falling due to the recession. The officers did not do any prior investigation as to how the re-pricing campaigns might affect their customers or the bank in the long term; they rejected historical experience, advice from bank management and consultants regarding their plan. They ignored more than 35,000 customer complaints the Bank received and Advanta's internal reports that repeatedly found issue with the re-pricing campaign.

At the end of 2007, Advanta Bank was in a very good position to survive the financial crisis, its customers' credit scores were among the highest in the field and all of its securitization Class A notes were rated AAA. The Bank had $420 million in capital and $1.029 billion in liquid assets. It was understood throughout the Bank that Defendants were in charge and in complete control of the management and operations of the Bank and the holding company. They were free to disregard warnings and advice from others; if someone disagreed with their strategy, they either left the Bank or were fired.

Defendants did hire an outside consultant, however the consultant had no experience in re-pricing campaigns and were given a perverse incentive to recommend increasing APRs: they were to receive 50% of any increased income from the proposed re-pricing. When their proposal was placed in front of the board for a vote, Defendants did not inform the members of the compensation incentive or of the consultants' lack of experience. In addition to the control Defendants exerted over the Bank and board, their lack of disclosure meant there was no meaningful understanding of the re-pricing campaign. Even so, there was near-unanimous objection from Bank management, two of whom were pushed out and replaced by people without bank officer or credit card re-pricing experience. The consultant's plan went forward and, later, Defendants created and implemented an even more aggressive re-pricing campaign.

As a result of the drastically increased APRs, approximately 400,000 customers closed their credit card accounts and left the bank, which caused an approximate net loss of $59 million. In addition, more than 40% of the remaining customers could not pay the increased rate and defaulted on the credit cards, causing an additional loss of approximately $140 million. In addition to financial losses caused by customers, the re-pricing campaign utilized deceptive and misleading notices: they did not disclose the fact or the amount of the increase, nor the reason for it, and did not give customers time to opt out. The FDIC found this amounted to gross negligence and a breach of fiduciary duties and resulted in an FDIC Restitution Order that cost the Bank $21 million.

FDIC as Receiver for Southern Community Bank v. Cameron
Filed June 18, 2013 in U.S. District Court for the Northern District of Georgia

The FDIC filed suit against eight former outside directors and one former inside director of Southern Community Bank alleging negligence and gross negligence. The bank failed on June 19, 2009. The FDIC seeks to recover $10.3 million.

In its complaint, the FDIC claims the following:

From the day Southern Community Bank opened in 1999, it pursued an aggressive growth strategy based primarily on CRE lending, especially ADC loans. From 2001 onward, the bank was over-concentrated in ADC loans and far exceeded its peer group. Defendants were aware of the risks inherent in this strategy; they knew it left them more vulnerable to fluctuations in the real estate market, but they did not properly mitigate those risks. The bank's loan policy was created in 2000 and updated in 2007. Defendants were aware of its provisions. Time and again, defendants violated the bank's loan policy, especially with excessive LTV ratios, imprudent lending practices, and regulatory warnings. Regulators specifically addressed high concentrations of CRE and ADC loans near the time Southern Community was founded and when it was pursuing its high-risk strategy; defendants ignored this advice. Defendants were aware of the declining real estate market but did not take proper measures to shield the bank from as much harm as they could. Instead, they continued lending into the depressed market.

231

FDIC as Receiver for Woodlands Bank v. Crowe
Filed July 15, 2013 in U.S. District Court for the
District of South Carolina

The FDIC filed a complaint against two directors, one inside and one outside, and one officer of Woodlands Bank, alleging negligence, gross negligence, and breach of fiduciary duty. The bank failed on July 16, 2010. The FDIC seeks to recover $6.3 million.

In its complaint, the FDIC asserts the following:

In 2007, Woodlands began opening new offices throughout the southeastern United States with a goal of rapidly increasing its assets. To aid this plan, defendants followed a high-risk growth strategy centered on CRE, ADC, and raw land loans, all of which are vulnerable to fluctuations in the real estate market. Between July 2007 and July 2009, defendants approved seventeen transactions. These loans were made after it was very clear the real estate market was collapsing and the global economy was teetering on the brink a crash. Defendants knew or should have known these transactions presented too much of a risk to the bank's future safety and stability. Not only was the general economic environment unstable, defendants did not follow the bank's loan policy or prudent lending practices; they repeatedly ignored regulator warnings and safe and sound banking practices. Additionally, Woodlands did not have a formal Loan Committee where directors came together to discuss the merits of each application. Instead, loans were generally presented and approved by email. That system bred a culture of disregard and lack of due care that defendants perpetuated.

FDIC as Receiver for Crescent Bank v. Boggus
Filed July 19, 2013 in U.S. District Court for the Northern District of Georgia

The FDIC seeks to recover $11 million from five former directors, both inside and outside, of Crescent Bank for negligence, gross negligence, and breach of fiduciary duty. The bank failed on July 23, 2010 and cost the DIF $297.5 million.

The FDIC asserts the following in its complaint:

In 2003, Crescent Bank's leadership decided they wanted to grow to $1 billion in assets by year-end 2007; one major way they planned to achieve this goal was through increased CRE and ADC lending. In those four years, the bank's loan portfolio increased by about 300%; CRE and ADC lending constituted a majority of that portfolio. Due to the increased risk CRE and ADC lending pose the bank, it is important that loans are made after careful deliberation and thoughtful consideration of their potential effect on the bank's health; defendants did not follow this maxim in their rapid expansion. Between November 2006 and March 2009, defendants approved six transactions, four CRE loans and two lines of credit, in clear violation of the bank's loan policy and prudent lending practices. There were distinct problems in the credit memoranda provided to defendants that made the risk of loss clear, but defendants approved the loans anyway.

The bank's loan policy was updated three times between 2005 and 2008, so defendants were clearly aware of its provisions and chose to ignore it. The loans they approved were not adequately underwritten, there was insufficient collateral, and the borrowers were not creditworthy. In addition, the economy was in shambles. The real estate bubble had burst and the market was experiencing swift decline, but defendants continued to make real estate loans without taking proper care. Defendants knew or should have known their behavior left the bank incredibly vulnerable.

FDIC as Receiver for Williamsburg First National Bank v. Chandler
Filed July 22, 2013 in U.S. District Court for the District of South Carolina

The FDIC seeks to recover $5.674 million from four former directors, both inside and outside, and two former officers of Williamsburg First National Bank for negligence, gross negligence, and breach of fiduciary duty. The bank failed on July 23, 2010.

The FDIC claims the following in its complaint:

Under defendant's direction, Williamsburg First National's asset growth between 2005 and 2007 far outstripped that of their peer group. Unfortunately, much of this growth was due to high-risk CRE and ADC loans made in contravention of the bank's loan policy and prudent lending practices. Sixteen loans that were made between August 2007 and August 2008 are illustrative of defendants' disregard for safe and sound banking practices and for their own internal lending policies. Seven of those loans were made after defendants were specifically warned by their regulators that it was essential they follow their loan policy and conduct careful financial analysis of their potential borrowers and guarantors; defendants did not follow these directions. Additionally, defendants were aware of the collapse of the real estate bubble, but they continued to lend into the disappearing market.

One loan officer defendant, McDonald, had an incredibly poor record of exceptions to the bank's loan policy. His record exceeded that of all other officers combined. As such, directors should have given his recommendations less weight and spent more time doing their own analysis of the loan applications he presented to the committee. They did not. The other two officer defendants were completely clueless about CRE and ADC lending and, in deference to their lack of experience, the loan committee should have exercised more care in reviewing their recommendations. Again, though director defendants were aware both of McDonald's poor record and the others' lack of knowledge or training, they gave weight to their recommendations. Defendants had a duty to preserve the safety and soundness of the bank; in approving these loans provided to them by parties they knew to be unreliable on inadequate information and in violation of bank loan policy and regulation, they violated that duty.

FDIC as Receiver for Wakulla Bank v. Dodson
Filed July 31, 2013 in U.S. District Court for the
Northern District of Florida

The FDIC seeks to recover $14 million from five former directors, both inside and outside, for negligence, gross negligence, and breach of fiduciary duty. The inside directors are being sued in their capacity as officers and only the three of them are liable for ordinary negligence. Wakulla Bank failed on October 1, 2010.

In its complaint, the FDIC asserts the following:

From 2002 to 2009, Wakulla Bank chose to implement an aggressive business plan focused on CRE and ADC lending. Defendants had personal knowledge of the risks associated with this type of lending and knew they should exercise increased care in reviewing and approving these loan applications. Instead of doing so, defendants repeatedly violated Wakulla's loan policy, bank regulations, and prudent, safe, and sound lending practices. Thirteen CRE and ADC loans approved by defendants are offered as evidence of their negligent practices in exercising their duties as members of the bank's loan committee. Defendants were aware of the declining real estate market but did not change their lending practices to reflect the new reality, they continued lending into a rapidly collapsing economy, which they knew or should have known would cause substantial damage to the bank.

One of the most glaring issues was that Wakulla lacked a Credit Underwriting Department. The bank created one in August 2009, but by then the damage was done and defendants had approved many loans on inadequate, incomplete, and inaccurate financial information; many of the loan presentation forms were clearly lacking information and detail, but defendants approved the loan anyway. The bank was repeatedly warned by regulators that its underwriting was deficient and that its portfolio was over-concentrated in CRE loans, but defendants did not take corrective action.

FDIC as Receiver for Ravenswood Bank v. Thorsen
Filed August 2, 2013 in U.S. District Court for the
Northern District of Illinois

The FDIC seeks to recover $9.14 million from eight former officers and inside and outside directors of Ravenswood Bank, alleging ordinary negligence of the officers and gross negligence and breaches of fiduciary duty for both officers and directors. Ravenswood failed on August 6, 2010.

The FDIC contends the following in its complaint:

Defendants devoted excessive amounts of bank capital to the Chicago real-estate sector and violated safe and sound banking practices, prudent lending policies, and the bank's own loan policy. Eight loans made between November 2005 and December 2008 exemplify this imprudent behavior. These eight loans were made after the FDIC and the IDFPR (the Illinois bank regulator) warned defendants that their practices and policies were risky; the regulators threatened enforcement action in order to ensure the bank returned to safe and sound footing. From early 2006 defendants received warnings from its compliance officer, regulators, and outside auditor that their over-concentration in CRE loans represented a serious risk to the bank's safety and soundness. Defendants were aware of the risks their increased exposure to the Chicago real estate market entailed and they had been repeatedly warned of a "bubble" in the real estate market; they continued to approve loans that they could not have reasonably believed would be repaid.

Ravenswood had a poor history with regulators. Since its opening in 1996, the bank had received a CAMELS rating of 3 four times. In 2003, when they were rated a 3, the examiners stated that it was due to their excessive concentration in risky real estate lending. They also found that Ravenswood was not following its loan policy. In 2004, FDIC proposed a Memorandum of Understanding. In it, they asked the board to reevaluate their loan process for CRE lending: requiring complete documentation, realistic loan repayment terms, and ensuring the borrower's financial information is current and supports the amount of credit extended. The board assured the FDIC that they would follow these guidelines but did not sign the MOU. They did amend Ravenswood's loan policy but did not change their lending practices to comply with the new loan policy and were again warned by the FDIC and Illinois bank regulator of the riskiness of their lending practices. By year-end 2008, the FDIC gave Ravenswood a CAMELS composite rating of 4 and presented the board with a Cease and Desist Order. Once again, the board was either unwilling or unable to comply with the Order. The next year, they received a composite CAMELS 5 rating. The bank failed just two weeks after the examination report was issued.

FDIC as Receiver for First State Bank v. Copenhaver
Filed August 6, 2013 in U.S. District Court for the Middle District of Florida

The FDIC filed suit against five former directors, one inside and four outside, and two former officers of First State Bank, alleging negligence, gross negligence, and breach of fiduciary duty. Only the officers are subject to allegations of ordinary negligence. First State failed on August 7, 2009. The FDIC seeks to recover $6.25 million.

In its complaint, the FDIC contends the following:

First State Bank embarked on an aggressive growth strategy based primarily on CRE and ADC lending in 2003, almost doubling the bank's loan portfolio in three years and concentrating about 70% of the bank's lending in high-risk CRE and ADC loans. Though defendants knew these loans represented a risk to the bank, they did not take increased precautions and, in fact, did not even take ordinary precautions. They did not follow First State's loan policy or prudent lending practices; they did not ensure proper repayment sources or the creditworthiness of borrowers. Instead, they recommended and approved loans without proper documentation and without adequate review. Defendants recommended and approved five non-conforming loans between November 2005 and May 2008. At the time the officers recommended some of those loans and directors approved them, the real estate market was in a steady decline. Defendants should have been more careful and taken more time to ensure these loans would not damage the bank; they did not, and continued their unspoken policy of utter disregard for First State's safety and soundness.

FDIC as Receiver for Affinity Bank of Ventura v. McGuire
Filed August 8, 2013 in U.S. District Court for the Central District of California

The FDIC filed a complaint against six former officers and three former outside directors of Affinity Bank, alleging negligence, gross negligence, and breaches of the fiduciary duties of care and loyalty. The bank's August 28, 2009 failure cost the DIF $297 million. The FDIC seeks to recover $52 million.

The FDIC asserts the following in its complaint:

Affinity Bank was not historically successful, until it changed its business plan to focus on CRE lending in 2000. From then on, the bank's loan portfolio grew rapidly and it turned a profit, but it became more concentrated in CRE loans. Affinity began to specialize in CRE and ADC lending, focusing almost solely on this loan category. Eight CRE and ADC loans, totaling more than $80 million, indicate defendants' complete disregard for the bank's loan policy and prudent lending practices in their quest for profit. Defendants' compensation was tied to growth in loan production rather than to the quality of the loans, so they had little incentive to do their due diligence and ensure the borrowers were creditworthy and the projects had sufficient collateral. As such, the borrowers were often in financial difficulty and the projects were poorly collateralized and poorly assessed. Additionally, defendants made loans outside the bank's normal lending area, which was relatively wide. Unsatisfied with their prospects in Affinity's familiar market, especially when the economy began to crumble, defendants began to approve loans throughout the country, which was expressly forbidden by the bank's loan policy. Defendants continued lending into the progressively deteriorating real estate market even after they became aware of the decline, which further demonstrates their focus on potential profit rather than the safety of Affinity Bank.

FDIC as Receiver for Shorebank v. Amy
Filed August 16, 2013 in U.S. District Court for the Northern District of Illinois

The FDIC filed suit against five former officers of Shorebank alleging ordinary and gross negligence and breach of fiduciary duty. Shorebank opened its doors in 1939; its failure, more than seventy years later, on August 20, 2010 caused a substantial loss to the DIF. The FDIC seeks to recover $73 million.

The FDIC contends the following in its complaint:

Shorebank had a loan policy that required adherence to the industry's prudent lending practices. In the twenty-eight instances detailed in the complaint, defendants did not adhere to the bank's loan policy or to safe and sound banking practices. The twenty-eight loans consist of twenty ADC loans, six commercial loans, and two CRE loans, all of which were approved between December 2005 and June 2009. Defendants failed to obtain up-to-date and accurate financial information from borrowers and guarantors, did not properly assess borrowers' ability to repay, did not obtain appraisals, and did not obtain proper committee approval, but approved loans anyway.

These loans were made in the face of a poor and deteriorating real estate market and, later, a falling global economy. Defendants knew or should have known of the increased risk this environment portended but they did nothing to lessen the bank's fatal exposure.

FDIC as Receiver for Butte Community Bank v. Ching.
Filed August 19, 2013 in U.S. District Court for the Eastern District of California

The FDIC brought a complaint against eleven of Butte Community Bank's ("Butte" or "the Bank") former officers and inside and outside directors, alleging ordinary negligence, gross negligence and breach of fiduciary duties. Butte failed on August 20, 2010 and the FDIC seeks to recover $8.8 million. Butte was wholly owned by Community Valley Bancorp ("CVB"), a California corporation, of which each of the defendants was also a director.

In its complaint, the FDIC alleges the following:

By 2007, it became clear the Butte was over-concentrated in risky real estate lending; this was seriously limiting the Bank's ability to grow in the increasingly bad market. With that in mind, the defendants decided to embark on a stock buyback in order to strip capital from the bank. They enlisted Sandler O'Neill, recognized specialists, in order to create a buyback program for the Bank and CVB. Sandler O'Neill created a five year stock buyback plan that allowed for flexibility to adapt to changing circumstances of the financial market. The defendants rejected that plan as too conservative and proceeded with their own plan, deciding against further outside consultation.

Defendants' plan differed in material respects from the plan created by Sandler O'Neill: it included a tender offer, a one-time purchase of one million CVB shares, and was executed in a quick series of transactions, as opposed to over five years. The plan primarily consisted of a Sale-Leaseback of seven buildings owned by Butte, which it sold and then immediately leased back; the cash from the sale was issued to CVB as a dividend, which CVB distributed to its shareholders participating in the tender offer (which included the majority of the defendants). This deprived the Bank of much-needed capital during a difficult time and constituted willful misconduct, negligence or gross negligence by the defendants. These directors either acted in their own self-interest as CVB stockholders in declaring the dividend and the tender offer or, in the alternative, they were behaving outside the bounds of prudence and reasonableness under the circumstances.

Nine of the eleven defendants participated in the tender offer, collecting a total of $3.7 million of the $13 million in proceeds. The investment banker they retained to help with the tender offer stated that, in his opinion, their share price of $13 was too high. The Bank's share price had been falling steadily since the onset of the Bank's overconcentration in CRE had come to light and the looming financial crisis was contributing to the falling numbers. The investment banker offered $11.50 as a fairer price, considering the publicly traded price was steadily falling and, on the day of the tender offer, it was trading at $9.99. The defendants were aware of the bank's overconcentration in real estate loans and knew that the bank was vulnerable, but they went ahead with the dividend. The dividend had an immediate adverse effect on Butte's regulatory capital.

The dividend funded by the lease-buyback violated both Butte's dividend policy and the Federal Reserve's policy. The Bank's policy stated that any dividend could not compromise the safety and soundness of the bank; this dividend did just that. The FRB's policy states that a bank cannot issue a dividend if it is based solely or largely upon a non-recurring event, like the sale-leaseback, if the funds could be better used to strengthen the bank's financial condition. In this case, the funds could certainly have been used to strengthen the bank's financial condition – after declaring the dividend, the bank was less than well-capitalized and, a month after the dividend and tender offer, CVB had to obtain a $4 million letter of credit from another bank in order to ensure Butte was not classified as such. Defendants' rationale for the dividend and tender offer was that Butte had excess capital. This was demonstrably untrue; CVB had to issue $8 million in preferred securities to the Bank in order to ensure it had enough cash on hand. To the contrary, the defendants knew Butte needed the capital, but they were heavily invested in CVB and wished to avoid potentially high losses on their investment. They placed their own self-interest above the safety and soundness of Butte.

FDIC as Receiver for Sonoma Valley Bank v. Switzer
Filed August 19, 2013 in U.S. District Court for the Northern District of California

The FDIC filed a claim against two former inside directors and one former officer of Sonoma Valley Bank alleging negligence, gross negligence, and breach of fiduciary duty. When the bank failed on August 20, 2013, the DIF suffered significant losses; the FDIC seeks to recover $12 million.

In its complaint, the FDIC makes the following allegations:

Defendants had a duty to ensure the soundness and stability of Sonoma Valley Bank and they did not fulfill that duty. Ten CRE loans and one commercial line of credit exemplify defendants disregard for their duties, the bank's loan policy, underwriting requirements and prudent lending practices.

Sonoma Valley Bank originally focused on making loans to small to medium-sized commercial businesses, professionals, and wealthier individuals around Sonoma, CA. However, in 2005 they changed their focus and decided to make CRE loans the focus of their loan portfolio. These loans were often outside the bank's territory and did not adhere to the bank's underwriting and loan policies. Each of the eleven loans offered as evidence had to be approved by both the Management Loan Committee and the Board Loan Committee, neither of whom fulfilled their obligations to engage in safe and sound banking and lending practices. Defendants knew or should have known that approving risky CRE loans in the face of a rapidly deteriorating real estate market would cause substantial losses to the bank. The bank's failure and loss of more than $12 million is due to defendant's derogation of their duties to Sonoma Valley Bank.

FDIC as Receiver for Security Bank of Bibb County v. Bridges
Filed September 16, 2013 in U.S. District Court for the Middle District of Georgia

Security Bank failed on July 24, 2009, causing the DIF to lose $358.9 million. The FDIC filed suit against sixteen former directors, three of whom were inside directors, claiming negligence and gross negligence. The FDIC seeks to recover $21.764 million in damages.

The complaint contends the following:

Defendants did not adhere to Security Bank's internal loan policy or to prudent lending and safe and sound banking practices. They disregarded their duty to make informed choices in approving loans over $3 million. Seven CRE and ADC loans and three lines of credit approved between August 2005 and April 2008 are offered as illustrative examples of the repeated lapses in defendants' duties to the bank. In addition to approving loans without adequate information or underwriting standards, defendants also loaned money to insiders under preferential terms and accepted loan participations from affiliate banks without doing proper due diligence on the underlying loans.

Regulators consistently warned defendants that the bank's portfolio was over-concentrated in high-risk CRE and ADC loans. Beginning in 2005, examinations and reports on the bank from multiple regulators consistently found the bank's lending practices of concern. In addition, defendants received a memo from independent consultants warning them of the slowdown in construction and "unforeseen deterioration in credit quality" in June 2006; they did not change their practices in response. By August 2006, they knew or should have known the real estate market was in significant decline, but they still did not change their practices to reflect the new, riskier situation. They continued to approve loans with deficient underwriting and without conducting due diligence or following federal and state regulations. Their portfolio was incredibly susceptible to changes in the housing market and their negligent practices led to catastrophic decline in the bank's asset quality from which it was not able to recover.

FDIC as Receiver for Centennial Bank v. Williams
Filed September 27, 2013 in U.S. District Court of Utah

The FDIC filed a complaint against three former officers and four former directors, one inside, of Centennial Bank, alleging negligence, gross negligence, and breach of fiduciary duty. When the bank failed on March 5, 2010, it cost the DIF $88 million. The FDIC seeks to recover $11.2 million.

In its complaint, the FDIC asserts the following:

Beginning in 2005, defendants knew or should have known that their policy of high concentration in risky and speculative CRE and ADC lending was dangerous for the bank. In 2005, they began to see losses from spec borrowers and received a report stating that the bank was over-dependent on the housing boom that was subject to "inevitable downturn." Defendants owed a duty to use care and diligence in approving loans and to keep the safety and soundness of the bank in focus; they did not perform their duties. Sixteen CRE and ADC loans approved between August 2006 and February 2008 show defendants' disregard for prudent, safe, and sound lending practices and the bank's internal lending policy. If defendants had exercised any prudence or done their due diligence, they would have seen these loans did not comply with the bank's lending policies: the documentation was insufficient, the underwriting was grossly inadequate, and the borrowers' sources of repayment were questionable. Defendants did not ask questions or request more complete information; they simply approved the loans.

The FDIC and Utah's bank regulator repeatedly warned defendants that Centennial's high concentration (90% of the bank's loan portfolio) of CRE and ADC loans meant they needed to heighten their standards for approval. Defendants did not heed the warnings and continued to make loans without sufficient information, underwriting, or risk management. Their over-concentration left the bank critically exposed to fluctuations in the real estate market, which did indeed have the "inevitable downturn" predicted in 2005.

FDIC as Receiver for Progress Bank of Florida v. Rummel
Filed October 18, 2013 in U.S. District Court for the Middle District of Florida

Progress Bank's October 22, 2010 failure cost the DIF $46.8 million. The FDIC seeks to recover $6.3 million from three directors, two of whom were outside directors. It alleges the director-officers were negligent and that all defendants were grossly negligent and breached their fiduciary duties.

The FDIC makes the following allegations in its complaint:

In 2007, the bank was acquired by a private equity firm, of which two defendants were limited partners. Defendants completely changed the bank's historical focus from residential lending to commercial lending, especially high-risk CRE and ADC loans. For almost twenty-five years, the bank had remained stable, though relatively small, focusing on local residential lending, but defendants wanted aggressive growth. From 2007 to 2009, Progress Bank's portfolio expanded exponentially: CRE lending went from $440,000 to $60.9 million; ADC lending went from 0 to $27.3 million. At the same time, and as a direct result, the bank's adversely classified assets ballooned from $1.3 million to $23.3 million. Defendants embarked on this aggressive growth strategy focused on real estate lending just as the housing market was rapidly declining nationwide, but especially in Florida. Defendants approved nine CRE and commercial loan transactions in this two year period that encapsulate the absolute disregard for market conditions, Progress

Bank's loan policy, prudent lending practices, and regulatory advice.

Not only was the bank lending into a market in free fall, defendants did not change their practices to reflect the increased risk of injury to the bank. Their underwriting was completely insufficient and did not rise to industry standards; defendants did not inform themselves of the specifics of the loans and the risk they represented; and they repeatedly ignored regulator warnings. The bank's high concentration in risky CRE and ADC lending was in direct violation of the FDIC's 2006 guidance on risk management in CRE lending and regulators repeatedly warned defendants of the risks associated with their growth strategies; defendants did not comply with regulatory advice or safe and sound banking practices. The plummeting real estate market caused catastrophic damage to the bank due to defendants' practices that left Progress Bank increasingly exposed to the whims of the market.

FDIC as Receiver for Hillcrest Bank of Florida v. Bayer
Filed October 22, 2013 in U.S. District Court for the Middle District of Florida

The FDIC filed a complaint against four former directors, three of whom were outside directors, of Hillcrest Bank alleging gross negligence. The inside director is also sued in ordinary negligence. The bank failed on October 23, 2009, causing the DIF to lose $47.7 million. The FDIC seeks to recover $7.487 million.

In its complaint, the FDIC alleges the following:

From its opening in August 2006 onward, the directors of Hillcrest pursued an aggressive growth strategy focused on making high risk CRE and ADC loans out of the bank's lending territory. This represented an immediate break with the business plan they had submitted to the FDIC in order to secure the bank's charter. The high concentration in risky loans was not outlined in Hillcrest's submitted business plan and, as such, their increased risk profile was not accounted for. Less than a year after opening Hillcrest, defendants were warned that they were not in compliance with the business plan or with the FDIC Order approving their deposit insurance; they ignored regulators warnings and continued their non-compliant strategies. Between August 2006 and June 2008, defendants approved nine transactions, including one approved the day after they opened for business, that illustrate their complete lack of due care and disregard for safe and sound banking practices, as well as their own stated policy. In approving the nine loans, defendants ignored serious deficiencies evident in the presentations; did not use adequate underwriting practices; and failed to adequately inform themselves of the potential risks involved in lending out of area in a volatile market. Defendants knew or should have known about the economic downturn and the turmoil in real estate markets, but they did not change their lending policies or underwriting practices to reflect the changing reality; in fact, they expanded their high-risk CRE and ADC lending practice while more prudent banks were contracting theirs. Defendants' disregard for prudent lending practices, safe and sound banking principles, and their own internal lending policy and business plan, left the bank critically exposed to the floundering real estate market. Despite repeated warnings from regulators, defendants did not change their practices to conform with lending practices commensurate with the risks they took.

FDIC as Receiver for Darby Bank v. Bowden
Filed November 8, 2013 in U.S. District Court for the Southern District of Georgia

Darby Bank failed on November 12, 2010, causing the DIF to lose $164.6 million. The FDIC seeks to recover $15.1 million from sixteen officers and inside and outside directors, claiming negligence, gross negligence, and breaches of fiduciary duty.

In its complaint, the FDIC makes the following allegations:

Darby Bank was a southern Georgia institution. It was founded in 1927 and operated on a small, community scale for many years until defendant Bowden took their reigns in 1995. He pursued an aggressive growth strategy: he expanded the bank's lending territory, increased CRE and ADC lending, and generally increased the bank's risk profile. From 1995 to 2008, the bank's assets increased from $55 million to $800 million. However, as early as 2004, regulators warned the board the bank was over-concentrated in CRE lending and the board needed to take action and refocus on loan quality. The bank's internal loan policy specifically addressed CRE and ADC loans and their inherent risk; defendants disregarded Darby's loan policy in approving thirty-three non-conforming, problematic loans between November 17, 2007 and October 26, 2009, which exemplify the negligent attitude defendants took towards their duties to the bank. Defendants on the Director's Loan Committee reviewed only the credit memoranda, summarizing the loan documents, and did not actually review or even receive the underlying documentation for the loans they approved. Regulators repeatedly warned that this practice was dangerously insufficient to safeguard against making bad loans. Defendants ignored them.

Darby Bank led its peer group in CRE loan concentrations and defendants were aware of the issue. In September 2007, CRE lending accounted for 707% of Tier 1 capital and ADC lending was 192% of Tier 1 capital. Darby's loan concentrations were far above those recommended by the interagency guidance released in 2006. In addition to excessive concentration, the loans were deteriorating rapidly and defendants did not take proper measures to counteract the damage, in fact, they renewed and extended loans and continued lending into an increasingly volatile market. By the time defendants approved the loans at issue here, they knew or should have known about the incipient economic downturn, especially in the local real estate market. Defendants did nothing to mitigate the risks and did not change their practices to reflect the changing economic reality; Darby Bank could not survive.

FDIC as Receiver for Oglethorpe Bank v. Cross-McKinley
Filed January 9, 2014 in U.S. District Court for the Southern District of Georgia

The FDIC has filed a complaint against eight former directors, five of whom were outside directors, alleging negligence, gross negligence and breaches of fiduciary duty in connection with the failure of Oglethorpe Bank. When the bank failed on January 14, 2011, it cost the DIF $98.2 million. The FDIC seeks to recover $9.88 million.

In its complaint, the FDIC makes the following allegations:

From its opening in August 2003, the bank's growth strategy was based on residential, CRE, and ADC loans. Oglethorpe's assets did grow quickly, but they were over-concentrated in CRE loans and had a high concentration of credit to a small number of developers. The bank did have an internal Loan Policy, one in keeping with safe and sound banking practices and prudent lending policies. However, the defendants did not follow it. They approved a total of twenty four loans detailed in the complaint that were poorly underwritten, not consistent with the bank's Loan Policy, and undermined the safety and soundness of Oglethorpe. Not only did defendants violate the bank's Loan Policy, they also violated their "Oath of the Bank Director", which all director defendants took in June 2006. In their Oath, they promised to "place the interests of the Bank before their own interests" and to "diligently and honestly administer the affairs of the Bank." They also stated their fiduciary role to the bank's shareholders and acknowledged their duties of loyalty and care.

In making the risky loans at issue here, defendants abdicated their duties to the bank and to the shareholders. Beginning in September 2004, regulators warned defendants that their underwriting process was insufficient. Loan underwriting practices are the predominant way in which a bank manages credit risk and loan portfolio risk. Defendants did not take adequate steps to address regulator's concerns about the deficient process. By 2007, it was clear that there were serious issues. Between 2006 and 2007, the bank's adversely classified assets had ballooned from $93,000 to $4.18 million, further increasing to $10.8 million in 2008. FIL 104-2006 addressed concentrations in CRE lending and how to properly manage the associated risks. In that Guidance, regulators clearly stated that they would consider banks with CRE concentrations of more than 300% of risk based capital or with ADC concentrations of more than 100% of risk based capital potentially in need of heightened risk-management practices. From 2007 to 2009, Oglethorpe's CRE concentration did exceed 300% of its risk based capital, but Defendants did not utilize the heightened risk-management practices required by the Guidance.

In early 2007, Defendants chose not to implement the recommendations of the independent loan consultants they had hired. The consultants warned Defendants in February and June 2007 that they needed to change their process in order to properly assess whether or not loans would be repaid. In 2010 one defendant admitted that they had not implemented the recommendations and that they had made bad loans without enough research. In 2008, Defendants were aware that Oglethorpe was in serious financial straits and received capital injections from its holding company, as well as, applying for TARP funds. Even though Defendants believed they needed government assistance, in 2009, Defendants approved the largest loan at issue in the complaint, which was made to another bank's holding company. Not only did Defendants fail to heed regulators' warnings about CRE and ADC concentrations and underwriting standards, but they also gave themselves expensive and unnecessary perks that amounted to a waste of bank assets. These included $278,000 in directors' fees in 2009, when the bank was not stable and the local and national financial and real estate markets were rapidly deteriorating; buying membership for all directors to the Brunswick Country Club; paying $30,000 for a directors' retreat to the Ritz Carlton, Amelia Island, Georgia; and paying for two defendants' memberships to the Sea Island Club.

In failing to heed warnings from the regulators, examiners, and consultants, Defendants broke their Oath, violated the bank's Loan Policy, as well as safe and sound banking principles and prudent lending practices. They wasted corporate assets lavishing themselves with gifts when the bank was unable to support itself. Even after they were definitely aware of the deteriorating market conditions locally and nationally, Defendants continued to approve loans that violated Oglethorpe's Loan Policy and regulatory guidance. They knew or should have known their actions would cause substantial losses to the bank, but they did not modify their behavior.

FDIC as Receiver for United Western Bank v. Berling
Filed January 17, 2014 in the U.S. District Court for the District of Colorado

United Western Bank failed on January 21, 2011. The FDIC has filed a complaint against six former directors (three outside) and three former officers of the bank, alleging negligence against the officers and inside directors, and gross negligence and breach of fiduciary duties against all defendants. The FDIC is seeking to recover $35 million in damages.

In its complaint, the FDIC contends the following:

United Western first opened in 1960 and served the New Mexico and Colorado regions, focusing mainly on single-family mortgages and small business loans. In 2005, the board brought in new management that changed the focus to ADC and CRE lending, hoping to quickly bolster the bank's earnings. United Western did grow quickly, but its portfolio was highly concentrated in the risky CRE and ADC lending area. Between March 2006 and March 2009, the Bank's CRE/ADC loan portfolio grew from 24% to 50% of total assets, constituting 605% of United Western's Tier 1 capital. In addition, the bank's adversely classified assets grew from $25.2 million in June 2007 to $70.3 million in March 2009. The bank had an internal Loan Policy that addressed commercial loans; for example, the loans had to be in the bank's market area (the Front Range of Colorado); could not be speculative (i.e. the repayment could not be dependent on the success of the speculative venture); and the borrower had to have the capacity to repay their loans. The FDIC supplies seventeen examples of loans made between November 2006 and August 2009 in violation of this Loan Policy as well as generally prudent lending practices.

Defendants not only disregarded their own Loan Policy and safe and sound banking principles, but also ignored warnings from various sources about the "softening" of the housing and real estate markets. As early as March 2006, Defendants received emails and reports about the probability of an impending economic downturn, especially in Colorado. Regulators also repeatedly warned Defendants of the riskiness of their highly concentrated CRE/ADC loan portfolio, which was worrisome even in good economic times. Defendants continued to increase United Western's concentrations in CRE and ADC loans and did not exercise the heightened scrutiny demanded by their Loan Policy, regulatory guidance, and generally prudent lending standards. Defendants approved loans that were non-conforming on their face and did not alter their behavior even after it became clear that the country was in the midst of a general financial downturn spurred, in part, by lax underwriting standards.

FDIC as Receiver for First Community Bank v. Dee
Filed January 23, 2014 in the U.S. District Court for the District of New Mexico

On January 28, 2011, First Community Bank failed, causing a loss to the DIF. The FDIC is seeking to recover more than $14.8 million from six inside directors and two officers, alleging negligence, gross negligence, and breaches of fiduciary duty.

The FDIC alleges the following in its complaint:

First State Bank of Taos (the name was changed to First Community Bank in 2005) opened for business in 1922. For eighty years, the bank stayed small and did not have regulatory issues. In 2002, the bank expanded into new, unfamiliar markets and changed into a production-driven culture, which resulted in high CRE, including ADC, loan concentrations. The focus changed to quick asset growth, which resulted in an alarming increase in adversely classified assets: between 2006 and 2009, the bank's adversely classified assets rose from $32 million to $538 million.

Defendants had a duty to engage in safe and sound banking principles and to follow all internal and applicable regulatory guidance. They did not do so. Defendants also improperly incentivized loan officers. They were rewarded based almost solely on production rather than on strength of the loan; the loan officers obliged. The FDIC offers six transactions (four CRE/ADC loans, one raw land, and one commercial business) made between January 29, 2007 and February 16, 2010 as illustrations of Defendants' disregard for their duties. These loans were made in violation of First

Community's internal Loan Policy, as well as prudent lending practices. They were poorly underwritten and made at a time when Defendants knew or should have known of the precarious condition of the real estate and financial markets, which should have given them greater pause. Instead, they placed the bank in an increasingly poor position relative to its peer group. Between 2007 and 2010, First Community was in the upper 90th percentile of its peer group in CRE-ADC loan concentration.

FDIC as Receiver for Tamalpais Bank v. Garwood
Filed January 27, 2014 in the U.S. District Court for the Northern District of California

The FDIC has filed a complaint against five former directors, one inside, and three former officers of Tamalpais Bank, alleging ordinary and gross negligence and breaches of fiduciary duty. On April 17, 2010, the bank failed with $611.5 million in assets. The FDIC is seeking to recover $20 million in damages.

The FDIC asserts the following in its complaint:

From its opening in 1991 until 2006, Tamalpais was run by its founder and CEO Kit Cole. She had no regulatory issues and the bank grew steadily. She stepped down in 2006 and the new leadership changed the business model, focusing on high-risk multi-family CRE lending, especially borrowers with a negative debt service coverage ratio (NDSCR). The bank's primary lending area was San Francisco and they heavily marketed the NDSCR program to mortgage brokers in that area. Defendants' presumption was that NDSCR borrowers would be able to pay back loans either by increasing rental income from the collateral property or by reselling the collateral at a profit. Beginning in 2007, examiners from the FDIC and the California regulator warned Defendants about the increased risk from high concentrations of CRE and NDSCR loans. In January 2008, the bank's former Chief Financial Officer warned the Board that "a severe liquidity strain throughout the entire system" would be especially detrimental to the bank considering its risky loan portfolio, but Defendants continued to expand their program through 2008. By March 31, 2009, the bank's CRE loan concentration was 969% of its Tier 1 capital, far exceeding the regulatory guidelines. At the same time, the bank's NDSCR loan concentration was 313% of its Tier 1 capital. To illustrate the distinct break with Ms. Cole's leadership, when the FDIC counted the delinquent loans in March 2009, 84% of the dollar amount came from loans made after Ms. Cole stepped down.

These loans were made with deficient underwriting procedures and were not in compliance with the bank's internal Loan Policy. The complaint has eighteen CRE loans made between April 2007 and October 2008 that exemplify Defendants' lack of due care and disregard for prudent lending practices and safe and sound banking principles. Fourteen of those loans, totaling more than $42 million, were made to a single family and its related entities and guarantors. This same family was the subject of a lawsuit by the San Francisco City Attorney's Office due to the poor conditions of its rental units and the poor treatment of its tenants. Other, larger banks had refused to lend or continue to lend to the family, but Tamalpais stepped into that void. The bank lost more than $13 million on those loans.

The bank had two Loan Policies during the relevant time: the 2006 Policy and the 2008 Policy. The 2006 Loan Policy called for general due diligence and adherence to prudent underwriting standards. In 2008, in acknowledgement of the bank's increasing business in the NDSCR lending area, the Loan Policy specified a minimum ratio of 0.8:1, meaning that the rents generated have to cover at least 80% of the debt repayment amount. Defendants did not follow either the 2006 Loan Policy or the more specific guidelines of the 2008 Policy. Some of the loans Defendants approved had NDSCRs in the 0.4:1 range and one was in the 0.3:1 range. Defendants' assumption that borrowers could increase rents or resell the collateral at a profit proved flawed as they consistently lost money in an increasingly perilous real estate market.

FDIC as Receiver for First Regional Bank v. Edwards
Filed January 28, 2014 in the U.S. District Court for the Central District of California

On January 28, 2010, First Regional Bank failed. The bank's collapse cost the DIF $522 million. The FDIC alleges that the negligence (only against the officers), gross negligence, and breaches of fiduciary duties of eleven former directors and officer is partly the cause of the failure. The FDIC seeks $72.46 million in damages.

The case was settled for $11.9 million in March 2014.

In its complaint, the FDIC asserts the following:

First Regional Bank always catered to a small, wealthy clientele. This strategy meant that the bank did not have very many accounts, but those that they had had very high average balances. Defendants decided to embark on a new growth strategy beginning in the early 2000s; they wanted to quickly grow profits and assets by focusing on risky CRE lending. For the first few years, this strategy was very successful: from 2002 to 2005, assets grew from $406 million to $1.81 billion. However, the growth was almost completely dependent on CRE loans, which constitutes 956% of the bank's Tier 1 capital by the end of 2005. Though First Regional did have an internal Loan Policy, it did not set concentration limits and Defendants did not follow it when approving loans anyway. Though the real estate market began to soften in early 2006, Defendants continued to approve large speculative CRE and ADC loans until mid-2007. The complaint gives ten examples of deficient, poorly underwritten loans made between December 8, 2005 and April 7, 2007. Defendants approved $138.98 million in loans that did not conform on their face with the Loan Policy or prudent lending practices. Defendants had been repeatedly warned by regulators that their lending practices exposed the bank to excessive risk. They ignored these warnings and continued to make decisions that put the bank in increasing danger.

By June 2008, the bank's CRE loan portfolio represented 1,119% of its Tier 1 capital, putting First Regional in the 99th percentile of its peer group. When these loans became non-performing, they swamped the bank very quickly: between December 2006 and December 2007, the bank's past-due loans grew from $500,000 to more than $23 million. By 2009, it grew to more than $400 million in past-due loans. Defendants could not save First Regional after their decision to ignore safe and sound banking principles and their own Loan Policy, which caused increasing losses and overwhelmed the bank.

FDIC as Receiver for Habersham Bank v. Stovall
Filed February 14, 2014 in the U.S. District Court for the Northern District of Georgia

The FDIC has filed a complaint against eight former directors and officers of Habersham Bank, alleging ordinary negligence, gross negligence, and breach of fiduciary duty. Habersham's failure on February 18, 2011 cost the DIF $141.1 million; the FDIC is seeking to recover $15.32 million.

In its complaint, the FDIC makes the following allegations:

After a century of operation, Habersham Bank changed its growth strategy and began to focus on CRE and ADC lending in the early 2000s. The bank had its own internal Loan Policy, which incorporated all of the relevant federal and state rules and guidance, along with guidelines specific to Habersham. Habersham also had its own internal Reg O Policy, which expanded upon the Fed's requirements under Regulation O. Defendants repeatedly violated the Loan Policy and regulatory guidance; the complaint details seven violative commercial real estate and other business loans they approved between February 28, 2007 and September 25, 2007.

Defendants had been put on notice by both the FDIC and the Georgia banking regulator that their increasing portfolio of CRE and ADC loans represented a grave risk to the bank. As early as 2004, regulators warned that Habersham's high concentration of ADC loans outstripped their peers and could be dangerous to the bank in a down economy. Each subsequent year, the bank's ADC concentration was higher and the regulators' warnings were harsher. In 2008, Habersham was downgraded to a CAMELS rating of 3; the examination report found that the high concentration of ADC loans (at that time equaling 460% of Tier 1 capital) was higher than the bank's peers and that Defendants needed to address asset quality issues, as well as ensuring adequate ALLL methodology. Throughout this period, Defendants did not adopt new guidelines or reduce their exposure to the high-risk ADC market. They continued to approve non-conforming loans to borrowers who were not credit-worthy. Defendants often renewed the bad loans they had made even though it was against the Loan Policy to renew a non-performing loan to renew a loan simply to move it from past due status or to loan money solely to pay the interest on a loan. Defendants did both.

In addition, Defendants authorized a stock repurchase and special dividend from Habersham to the single-bank holding company, which had the same board of directors. On October 20, 2007, when Defendants were aware of the real estate downturn, they unanimously voted to award a $4.1 million dividend from the bank to the holding company. This was in addition to $1.2 million, which had been approved and distributed earlier in 2007. The two dividends outstripped the bank's net income for 2007 by $1.35 million. Defendants knew that the bank was overexposed to the quickly deteriorating real estate market and still voted to drain Habersham of cash during this precarious time.

FDIC as Receiver for Bradford Bank v. Arthur
Filed February 28, 2014 in the U.S. District Court for the District of Maryland

The FDIC has filed a complaint against four former officers and directors, two outside, of Bradford Bank alleging negligence, gross negligence, and breaches of fiduciary duty. Bradford failed on August 28, 2009. The FDIC is seeking $7.43 million in damages.

The FDIC contends the following in its complaint:

For more than one hundred years, Bradford Bank was a small institution focused on traditional community banking and served the Baltimore area. In 2005, though, Defendants changed the bank's growth strategy and long-term goals. The President wanted to convert the bank into a public stock institution and believed the best strategy to achieve the goal was to quickly grow the bank's assets – he wanted to grow that bank's assets to $1 billion in three years. Part of the argument in favor of the conversion was that Defendants would personally make a lot of money quickly by making Bradford a public stock corporation. In order to achieve this growth, Defendants pursued an aggressive growth strategy focused primarily on CRE and ADC loans. Though the real estate market was softening in early 2006 and falling in 2007, Defendants continued to blindly follow their strategy. The complaint details seven loans approved between March 2006 and October 2007 that did not comply with Bradford's internal Loan Policy or with principles of safe and sound banking. The Loan Policy incorporated all regulatory guidelines and requirements, as well as making specific provisions for high-risk CRE and ADC lending – namely, even more stringent underwriting policies and requirements of developers' equity in the proposed development. However, Defendants did no heed their own policies and approved millions in loans that were deficient on their face. Had Defendants adequately performed their duties, they would have heeded their own policies and regulatory guidance and would not have exposed Bradford to the increasingly perilous economic downturn.

FDIC as Receiver for Century Security Bank v. McClung
Filed March 14, 2014 in the U.S. District Court for the Northern District of Georgia

Century Security Bank failed on March 19, 2010. The FDIC is seeking $6.39 million in damages from six former officers and directors, four of whom were outside directors, alleging negligence, gross negligence, and breach of fiduciary duties.

The FDIC alleges the following in its complaint:

From its inception on February 28, 2006, Century Security Bank focused on CRE and ADC lending in higher concentrations than their initial business plan allowed. In their application for a charter, Defendants claimed they would focus on commercial, CRE, and ADC loans but that they would constitute, at a maximum, 28%, 35%, and 30%, respectively, of total loans. By 2009, CRE and ADC loans accounted for 73% of Century's total loans. Additionally, the bank's business plan stated that, by 2008, core deposits would account for 55% of total deposits. Throughout its four years of existence, core deposits never accounted for more than 10% of the bank's total deposits. Though the bank had a Loan Policy that incorporated all relevant federal and state guidance and more specific guidelines regarding CRE lending and student loans, Defendants violated the Loan Policy almost immediately after opening. Bank examiners repeatedly warned Defendants that their actions placed the bank in danger and they needed to have more robust underwriting procedures. Defendants ignored the regulators. The bank did not even have a Senior Loan Officer to supervise the lending function until March 2008. The complaint identifies seven transactions between July 2006 and December 2009 in which Defendants clearly disregarded Century's Loan Policy and prudent lending practices.

Six of the loans are CRE and ADC loans and one is the purchase, for more than $2.31 million, of a student loan pool in December 2009. The bank was in serious trouble, having received a cease and desist order from the Georgia bank regulator in 2008. In a last ditch attempt to turn the failing bank around, Defendants approved the purchase of 42 foreign student loans to a medical school in the Caribbean that had only just received its accreditation. This purchase violated an express provision of the Loan Policy, namely that the bank was not to have anything to do with student loans. This non-conforming, deficient loan is indicative of Defendants' lack of due care in running the bank and their disregard of general principles safety and soundness.

FDIC as Receiver for McIntosh Bank v. Burson
Filed March 14, 2014 in the U.S. District Court for the Northern District of Georgia

The FDIC has filed a complaint against eight former officer and directors, five of whom were outside directors, alleging negligence, gross negligence, and breach of fiduciary duties. McIntosh Bank failed on March 26, 2010 and has cost the DIF $171.4 million. The FDIC is seeking $12.03 million in damages.

In its complaint, the FDIC contends the following:

McIntosh Bank failed after less than ten years in operation. The bank opened in 2002 and by 2006, Defendants decided to pursue an aggressive growth strategy in order to more than double their total assets by 2012. In order to achieve that goal, Defendants focused on CRE and ADC lending in high concentrations. As they were discussing the strategy, the FDIC released its proposed guidance on CRE lending and issued the final guidance, with particular focus on limiting CRE and ADC concentrations in December 2006. Defendants dismissed the FDIC's guidance and ignored their own internal Loan Policy in favor of approving loans that were inherently risky without taking the necessary precautions. The complaint details eleven loans and loan participations approved by Defendants between March 21, 2006 and June 19, 2007. Though both general principles of prudent lending and safe and sound banking, as well as their own Loan Policy, required Defendants to take account of the general economic climate, they did not do so and continued to loan into an increasingly unstable economy. Not only did Defendants not adjust their actions to better reflect the troubling economic times, but they consistently approved loans that did not conform to their Loan Policy or regulatory requirements. Defendants approved loans before the required documentation was available to them; they accepted unsupported appraisals and out of date financial statements. In addition, the Market Chairman and Commercial Lending Officer, who was fired in 2009, lied on the loan reports – both about his own involvement in some deals or about his knowledge of certain deals. After years of Defendants disregarding regulatory guidance and warnings from examiners, the adversely classified assets and non-performing loans overwhelmed McIntosh and the bank failed.

FDIC as Receiver for Superior Bank v. Hall
Filed April 9, 2014 in the U.S. District Court for the
Middle District of Florida

The FDIC has filed a complaint against twelve former directors (four outside, three inside) and officers of Superior Bank claiming negligence (solely against the officer defendants), gross negligence, and breach of fiduciary duty. The bank's April 15, 2011 failure caused a loss to the DIF and the FDIC is seeking to recover at least $44 million.

In its complaint, the FDIC makes the following allegations:

Superior Bank was chartered in 1957 as Warrior Savings Bank. In 2005, when it was operating as The Bank, Superior changed its strategy to focus on high-risk real estate lending in Florida. In 2006, when it changed its name to Superior Bank, the strategy was in place and lending was growing. Between 2007 and 2010, Superior's CRE portfolio increased from 342% of capital plus reserves to 662%. The bank was dangerously over-concentrated in CRE and ADC lending and Defendants knew that this strategy involved heightened risk but did not take the requisite measures to protect the bank. Superior had an internal Loan Policy that called for robust underwriting procedures and for any loans to insiders to be made on substantially similar terms as those made to outsiders; Defendants flagrantly violated this Policy. They approved multiple multi-million dollar loans to insiders on far more preferential terms and subsequently lost millions of dollars on those deals. Between December 2007 to June 2009, Superior's classified assets increased by more than 141%, from $156.9 million to $378.2 million. The FDIC offers fourteen transactions made between 2007 and 2010 as illustrative examples of Defendants' complete disregard of the bank's own Loan Policy, safe and sound banking principles, prudent lending practices, as well as the generally deteriorating economic condition.

FDIC as Receiver for Bartow County Bank v. Akin
Filed April 14, 2014 in U.S. District Court for the
Northern District of Georgia

Bartow County Bank failed on April 15, 2011, which caused a substantial loss to the DIF. The FDIC filed suit against five directors, four of whom were outside directors, and one officer. They are seeking damages in an amount to be proven at trial.

The FDIC alleges the following in its complaint:

Bartow County Bank began operating in 1973 and grew gradually, expanding to four locations in northwest Georgia over thirty years. The bank had always focused on traditional community banking, but in 2006 that changed. Bartow County Bank began to make risky CRE and ADC loans. Between 2006 and 2009, the bank's CRE and ADC loan portfolio increased from $139 million to $152 million and its overall assets increased from $332 million to $427 million. The bank's internal loan policy had strict requirements for making CRE and ADC loans. In making the seven loans listed in the suit, the members of the loan committee failed to follow the bank's internal loan policy, as well as prudent lending practices and relevant regulations. In doing so, they violated their fiduciary duties and were negligent and grossly negligent. The seven loans were approved throughout 2007, when the real estate market was already unstable and even though the borrowers were not compliant with the bank's requirements.

FDIC as Receiver for First Banking Center v. Beere
Filed May 20, 2014 in U.S. District Court for the Eastern District of Wisconsin

The FDIC has filed a complaint against twelve former directors, two of whom were inside directors, of First Banking Center claiming negligence (under Wisconsin law) and gross negligence. The FDIC is seeking to recover $11.8 million from the former directors. The FDIC is also suing Travelers Insurance Company for the remaining proceeds from the D&O policy to cover losses; it is seeking to recover $4 million from Travelers.

In its complaint, the FDIC contends the following:

The bank opened in 1920 and for 85 years its commercial clients were limited to small business owners and farmers located in southeast Wisconsin. In 2005 though, the board embarked on an aggressive growth strategy focused on CRE and ADC lending, both inside and outside of the bank's traditional lending area. The bank's assets grew rapidly, from $663 million in 2005 to $930 million by the end of 2008. However, by March 31, 2007, the bank's CRE loans represented 407% of its total risk-based capital ($281 million), which exceeded regulatory guidelines and placed First Banking Center at the top of its peer group. Because CRE and ADC lending is riskier than the traditional lending the bank had previously done, Defendants needed to increase risk management and hire specialists. They did not. Not only did Defendants not implement heightened risk management guidelines for CRE and ADC lending; they did not even follow the bank's internal Loan Policy in approving all these risky loans. The bank's Loan Policy required compliance with the Commercial Lending Procedures Manual, which specifically addressed commercial loans and was relatively conservative in its requirements for approval. The complaint provides seven examples between December 2006 and May 2008 wherein Defendants disregarded the Loan Policy, including the Commercial Manual, and prudent lending practices, lending millions for speculative projects. Six of the seven loans were actually just to two borrowers for two development projects – Defendants continued to lend into increasingly costly projects over a period of years, even in deteriorating economic conditions.

FDIC as Receiver for Atlantic Bank and Trust v. Barone
Filed May 30, 2014 in U.S. District Court for the District of South Carolina

Atlantic Bank and Trust failed on June 3, 2011, causing a substantial loss to the DIF. The FDIC has filed a complaint alleging negligence, gross negligence, and breach of fiduciary duty against seven former officers and directors of Atlantic. The FDIC is seeking to recover $9.263 million.

In its complaint, the FDIC contends the following:

Atlantic Bank and Trust was established in 2006 and, from the beginning, Defendants pursued an aggressive and unsustainable growth strategy based on increasing CRE, raw land, and ADC lending. Though Defendants knew or should have known that such a high-risk lending strategy required heightened risk management and underwriting, they did not implement such procedures. Examiners repeatedly warned Defendants that the bank's concentration of CRE, ADC, and land loans was too high; Defendants did not alter their strategy or implement any new procedures to mitigate risk. Their disregard for prudent lending practices, the bank's own Loan Policy, and safe and sound banking principles is illustrated by twenty two loans made by Atlantic between June 2008 and April 2009. Defendants repeatedly disregarded the Atlantic's Loan Policy and approved loans that were outside their lending authority, including insider loans. They approved loans that were facially deficient based on the Credit Memoranda; they approved loans to

borrowers they knew or should have known did no
have the ability to repay. Defendants continued
approving bad loans well into the recession when it was
clear that the real estate market and general economy
were faltering badly. Atlantic never made a profit. The
bank's adversely classified assets jumped exponentially
from $0 in June 2007 to $43.2 million in December 2010.

FDIC as Receiver for Integra Bank v. Vea
Filed July 25, 2014 in U.S. District Court for the
Southern District of Indiana

Integra Bank's July 29, 2011 failure caused the DIF to lose at least $227 million. The FDIC is seeking to recover at least $32 million from six former officers of Integra. The FDIC alleges they were negligent, grossly negligent, and breached their fiduciary duties in the operation and management of the bank.

The FDIC asserts the following in its complaint:

Integra Bank had performed traditional community banking activities for the Evansville, Indiana region since 1850. In 2003, however, its leadership decided to adopt a new growth strategy focused largely on CRE lending. Their pursuit of growth included geographic expansion – the bank opened Loan Production Offices, focused on CRE lending, in Louisville, Chicago, Cincinnati, and Cleveland, which were overseen by one of the defendants. Between 2003 and 2008, Integra rapidly expanded its CRE portfolio. This growth came at the expense of prudent lending practices. In 2007 and 2008, Integra outpaced its peer group in CRE loan concentration and was significantly over the FDIC's recommended concentration limit of 300%. In June 2007, the bank's CRE concentration was at 316%, but by December 2008, it had grown to 436%.

Defendants were tasked with ensuring that the bank's internal policies were enforced, as well as following general safe and sound banking practices. They did neither. Integra had a strict internal Loan

Policy that would have ensured prudent underwriting and a robust loan approval process. Defendants routinely ignored this Policy. Eleven loan transactions made between September 2005 and May 2008 illustrate Defendants' disregard for Integra's Loan Policy, as well as prudent lending practices and safe and sound banking policies, in general. Many of these loans were approved despite Defendants lacking the authority to do so. Others were approved for construction projects far outside the bank's traditional lending area, including Florida and Arizona. In addition, Defendants consistently approved loan increases after borrowers had already demonstrated an inability to pay. The applications were facially deficient and Defendants knew or should have known that approving these loans would jeopardize the safety and soundness of the bank.

FDIC as Receiver for BankMeridian v. Houser
Filed July 28, 2014 in U.S. District Court for the District of South Carolina

BankMeridian failed on July 29, 2011. The FDIC is seeking to recover compensatory damages from nine former officers and directors of the bank. It alleges the former officers (and inside directors in their capacity as officers) were negligent and grossly negligent. The former outside directors of the bank were allegedly grossly negligent and breached their fiduciary duty.

In its complaint, the FDIC claims the following:

BankMeridian was founded in 2006 and from inception its leadership pursued a growth strategy focused on high-risk CRE and ADC loans. It was a successful strategy: between June 2006 and June 2008, the bank's assets grew from $49.2 million to $265.4 million. However, Defendants repeatedly ignored prudent lending practices, safe and sound banking policies, and their own Loan Policy in order to achieve this impressive growth. Defendants continued to make these high risk loans even after it became clear that the regional and national real estate market was declining precipitously. By September 2008, BankMeridian significantly outpaced its peer group in CRE concentrations; its CRE portfolio totaled 416% of the bank's total capital, placing it in the 89th percentile of its peer group. Defendants' lax view of judicious underwriting and approval procedures are illustrated by nine loans approved between December 2006 and April 2009. These loans include seven CRE and ADC loans, one refinancing loan secured by bank stock, and one yacht loan. Some of the loans were made out of the bank's traditional lending area; two of the loans were insider loans that violated both Reg. O and the bank's Loan Policy; one loan was approved with a self-prepared valuation from the borrower; and many were approved with deficient paperwork, especially inadequate or outdated appraisals.

FDIC as Receiver for First Bank of Idaho v. Coleman
Filed July 29, 2014 in U.S. District Court for the
District of Idaho

First Bank of Idaho failed on April 24, 2009, causing a substantial loss to the DIF. The FDIC has filed a complaint against four former officers of the bank, alleging negligence, gross negligence, and breach of fiduciary duties. The FDIC seeks to recover at least $11 million in damages.

In its complaint, the FDIC asserts the following:

First Bank had a robust internal Loan Policy that took into account all applicable laws and regulations and prescribed strict procedures for the underwriting and eventual approval of each loan. Defendants routinely ignored the Loan Policy and generally prudent lending practices. Their lack of care is exemplified by three loans made between May 2005 and January 2007. Defendants did not attempt to do the necessary due diligence to ensure that the bank's loan committee knew of any deficiencies in the application or the applicant for a loan. Due to First Bank's incentive pay structure, one defendant received a loan origination bonus that was nearly 25% of his salary. The loans were poorly underwritten; important facts were buried in the Credit Memo; and the defendant left the bank soon after receiving his bonus. Defendants recommended loans with deficiencies obvious to anyone who cared to look – including one to a borrower who had recently been convicted of felony wire fraud and stock manipulation.

FDIC as Receiver for First National Bank of Olathe v. Lindamood
Filed August 8, 2014 in U.S. District Court for the District of Kansas

The FDIC has filed a complaint against eleven former officers and directors, six of them outside directors, and the former Chief Loan Officer of First National Bank of Olathe. The complaint alleges that former officers (and inside directors sued in their capacity as officers) were negligent, grossly negligent and breached their fiduciary duties. The outside directors and Chief Loan Officer were allegedly grossly negligent and breached their fiduciary duties. Olathe failed on August 12, 2011, causing the DIF to lose approximately $121.3 million. The FDIC is seeking to recover $19.93 million.

In its complaint, the FDIC makes the following assertions:

Beginning in 2003, the bank changed course and begin to pursue an aggressive growth strategy centering on increasing CRE lending. Defendants knew or should have known that CRE lending is a high risk strategy and requires increased risk management policies and supervision; they did not implement such policies. In addition, Defendants knew or should have known that excessive concentration in any one asset is dangerous to the health and stability of a bank. They ignored both regulatory guidance related to CRE loan concentrations and safe and sound banking practices. Olathe had an internal Loan Policy that required strict underwriting, the enforcement of all relevant regulatory rules and guidance, as well as general prudent lending policies. Defendants revised the Loan Policy frequently between December 2006 and August 2009, but they consistently ignored it when approving loans. Six loans made between December 2007 and August 2009 are illustrative of Defendants' dismissive attitude toward Olathe's Loan Policy, prudent lending policies generally and safe and sound banking practices. These loans include a multi-million dollar loan to build a large airplane hangar with no analysis of whether or not the region had any demand for such a project; it did not. Additionally, Defendants extended loans simply to eliminate borrowers' past-due status and consistently did not follow their own approval procedures.

FDIC as Receiver for Bank of the Commonwealth v. Woodard
Filed September 19, 2014 in U.S. District Court for the Eastern District of Virginia

The FDIC has filed a complaint against ten former directors, nine of whom were outside directors, alleging negligence, gross negligence, breach of fiduciary duties as well as negligent and grossly negligent failure to adequately supervise the bank's lending and breach of fiduciary duty for failure to adequately supervise the bank's lending. Bank of the Commonwealth failed on September 23, 2011. The FDIC is seeking to recover $11.4 million.

In its complaint, the FDIC alleges the following:

Bank of the Commonwealth opened in 1970 and grew steadily in the Hamptons Road region of Virginia and northeastern North Carolina. In 2006, the board of directors announced its "Billion Dollar Builder Promise." This "Promise" entailed an aggressive lending strategy focused on CRE loans to grow the bank's assets to $1 billion in three years. They accomplished their goal – by 2008, the bank had $1.3 billion in assets, but they had achieved that benchmark at the expense of safety and soundness. The board of directors did not implement the necessary policies and procedures to handle the increased concentration on specialized CRE and ADC loans. Eleven loans approved by Defendants between February 2008 and July 2010 are illustrative of Defendants' lax attitudes toward risk management and prudent lending.

The bank's own Loan Policy called for strict underwriting and prudent lending practices. Defendants ignored both their internal Loan Policy and safe and sound lending practices. Beginning in 2006, regulators criticized the bank's loan documentation as incomplete; as Defendants proceeded with their Billion Dollar Builder Promise regulators grew more alarmed. By 2007, examiners stated that the bank's risk management policies needed immediate attention; they were ignored. In 2008, regulators warned that the bank's goal of aggressive asset growth was undermining prudent underwriting and safe and sound lending practices; they noted, especially, the increasingly prevalence of incomplete credit memoranda, which left the bank with only a partial picture of their borrowers. These same warnings were repeated in 2009. Defendants did change their internal Loan Policy in 2009 to comport with new regulations (such as new maximum LTV ratios for CRE loans) and to show regulators that they were paying attention. However, Defendants ignored the new Loan Policy once it was in place and continued to approve facially deficient, imprudent loans. They approved an insider loan that violated Regulation O; they approved multiple loans to borrowers they knew or should have known did not have the ability to repay; and they approved loans that resulted in over-concentration in certain borrowers. Defendants continued to make speculative CRE and ADC loans when it was clear that the real estate market and general economy were declining.

FDIC as Receiver for Blue Ridge Savings Bank, Inc. v. Taylor
Filed October 10, 2014 in U.S. District Court for the Western District of North Carolina

The FDIC has filed a complaint against two former directors, one of whom was also an officer. In the complaint, they allege negligence, gross negligence, and breach of fiduciary duties. Blue Ridge Savings Bank failed on October 11, 2011; the loss to the DIF is currently estimated at $47.3 million. The FDIC is seeking to recover $7.583 million. Further, Defendants' decisions are not shielded by the Business Judgment Rule because they did not avail themselves of readily available and material information to inform their decisions and as such, their choices are not the product of a rational process.

The FDIC makes the following allegations in its complaint:

Blue Ridge was 99.9% owned by its Chairman of the Board, the non-officer director Defendant, and he exercised control over the bank's actions and its general direction. Blue Ridge was chartered in 1978 in Asheville, North Carolina. It slowly grew to operate ten branches in the Asheville area. Defendants began focusing more and more on CRE and ADC loans. Despite receiving the Interagency Guidance stating that banks with CRE concentrations of above 300% risk-based capital would be considered significant exposure risks and require heightened risk management practices, the bank became more and more concentrated in CRE loans. It far surpassed its peer group in CRE concentration; CRE loans consistently made up 600% of the bank's total capital and once accounted for 785% of total capital. Defendants were aware of their standing in their peer group and of the fact that their CRE portfolio placed them in the "significant exposure" category, but they did not alter their behavior or implement heightened risk management practices. Fourteen loans Defendants approved between December 5, 2005 and September 11, 2008 demonstrate their disregard for Blue Ridge's Loan Policy, as well as prudent lending practices. The Loan Policy was amended no less than sixteen times between November 2005 and November 2008, though Defendants' behavior in approving facially deficient loans did not change. At first, the Loan Policy made general statements of compliance with prudent lending practices, but did not specify the processes necessary to achieve compliance; Defendants represented to their regulator, OTS, they did have specific requirements and processes in place.

The Loan Policy allowed for loans to be underwritten using "alternative documentation," which meant the loan committee reviewed twelve months of bank statements to approximate income and assets rather than reviewing the borrower's previous two years' W2s, a credit report, and employment verification, among others. Though the Loan Policy stated "alternative documentation" would only be allowed on a limited, case-by-case basis, Defendants used it frequently, especially in the fourteen loans at issue. The Loan Policy also called for the loan officer to prepare an in-depth credit memorandum detailing the borrower and guarantor's sources of funds, repayment sources, strengths and weaknesses of credit, and total credit exposure. The credit memoranda for the fourteen loans were one page and handwritten, and while some identified potential areas of weakness, including the "housing bubble," they were not in-depth analyses of the borrowers or guarantors. Moreover, Defendants even approved loans before receiving these typically deficient credit memoranda and ignored the potential weaknesses of the borrowers when they were documented. Defendants repeatedly ignored the bank's Loan Policy, prudent lending practices, their Chief Credit Officer (who was fired in June 2008), the OTS, and their outside loan reviewer. Due to their overconcentration in the risky CRE and ADC lending market, they were too exposed to recover from the economic downturn.

FDIC as Receiver for Mid City Bank, Inc. v. Fitl
Filed November 3, 2014 in U.S. District Court for the District of Nebraska

Mid City Bank failed on November 4, 2011. The FDIC has brought suit against the bank's former President and Chairman of the Board, alleging he was grossly negligent and breached his fiduciary duties. The FDIC is seeking to recover $4.018 million.

In its complaint, the FDIC contends the following:

Defendant had been Chairman of the Board and President of the bank since the early 1970s and he dominated Mid City. He was also a large shareholder in the bank's holding company. The bank had a written Loan Policy, but it was sparse on details. It made general statements regarding compliance but did not actually dictate the bank's requirements regarding debt-to-income ratios, loan-to-value ratios, or other documentation necessary to prudent underwriting and lending practices. The Loan Policy did not even require written documentation for approval or standard written credit/ loan memoranda until it was rewritten in August 2009 with much more detail. It was not until August 2009 that the bank had a Loan Committee to review and approve loans; prior to that date, Defendant had approved loans, often orally. This general disregard for prudent lending practices and safe and sound banking policies is demonstrated in seventeen loans approved by Defendant between July 2007 and March 2010. Twelve were commercial loans and five were commercial real estate loans; all loans at issue were made to two borrowers. Defendant approve these loans to the two borrowers without proper documentation, without analyzing their ability to repay, without performing a cash flow analysis, or even getting tax returns or financial statements from the borrowers. Further, the majority of the loans were made to rewrite previous loans made to the borrowers without confirming the borrowers had proper collateral or whether or not they had any other liens. While the Mid City Bank Loan Policy was seriously lacking in detail, these loans still violated it, as well as showing a lack of even slight care for compliance with safe and prudent banking practices.

APPENDIX I

BANK FAILURE STUDIES

LESSONS TO BE LEARNED

There have been a number of post mortems on bank failures. There was a bumper crop following the rash of bank and thrift failures in the late 1980's and early 1990's (the "S&L crisis"). For bank failures since 2009, there have been numerous Material Loss Reviews conducted by the Inspectors General of the FDIC, Federal Reserve, and Department of Treasury.

The studies conducted on the reasons for the bank and thrift failures during and after the S&L crisis can be of help to bank directors. Bank directors are often the means by which a potentially failing bank is turned around before it fails. Effective bank directors can identify the signs of a bank at risk early on, and thereby have time to take corrective action. Learning the characteristics of a failed bank can be helpful. It gives the bank director insight into the causes of bank failures, and what to look for in their institutions at an early stage.

An essential tool as an early warning system for bank boards of directors is the use of red flags. See OCC's "Detecting Red Flags in Board Reports – A Guide for Directors" (February 2004, reprint September 2013).
http://www.occ.gov/publications/publications-by-type/other-publications-reports/Detecting-Red-Flags.pdf.

Following the S&L crisis, the Comptroller of the Currency adopted a "Canary System" for its examiners to use to determine at an early stage whether a bank was in danger of failing. It was aptly named because it is the canary that is placed in coal mines to measure, before it is too late, whether there is any lethal gas in the air that will endanger the coal miner. One of the resources listed below is the OCC's "An Examiner's Guide to Problem Bank Identification, Rehabilitation and Resolution". While it is designed for use by national bank examiners, it is also a very valuable resource for bank boards of directors and bank management to help them identify problems early.

Studies on Bank and S&L Failures During the S&L Crisis:

Here are some of the studies that evaluated the bank and S&L failures of the late 1980's and early 1990's:

1. The Changing Business of Banking: A Study of Failed Banks from 1987 to 1992. Congressional Budget Office, Washington, D.C. 1994. Prepared at the request of the Senate Banking Committee, the study examined the major factors contributing to bank failures during the period outlined and discussed the extraordinary resolution costs that resulted.
www.cbo.gov/showdoc.cfm?index=4915&sequence=0.

2. History of the Eighties: Lessons for the Future. FDIC, Washington, D.C. 1998.
www.fdic.gov/bank/histroical/history/vol1.html

3. <u>Origins and Causes of the S&L Debacle: A Blueprint for Reform</u>, National Commission on Financial Institution Reform, Recovery, and Enforcement, GPO, Washington, D.C. July 1993.

4. <u>Bank Failure: An Evaluation of the Factors Contributing to the Failure of National Banks</u>, Office of the Comptroller of the Currency, Washington, D.C. 1988.
    <u>www.occ.treas.gov/bankfailure.pdf</u>

5. <u>An Examiner's Guide to Problem Bank Identification, Rehabilitation, and Resolution</u>, OCC, Washington, D.C. January 2001. <u>www.occ.treas.gov/prbbnkgd.pdf</u>

6. <u>Compendium Report, Safety, Soundness, and Accessibility of Financial Services: Summary of Treasury OIG's Material Loss Reviews of Failed National Banks and Thrift Institutions between 1993 and 2002</u>, Office of Inspector General, Department of Treasury, OIG-CA-04-004.
    <u>www.ustreas.gov/offices/inspector-general/evaluation-reports/ca04004.pdf</u>

7. <u>Bank Failure Report, An Evaluation of the Factors Contributing to the Failure of National Banks</u>, Office of the Comptroller of the Currency, June 1988. occ.gov/publications/publications-by-type/other-publications-reports/pub-other-bank-failure.pdf

Other Bank Failure Studies:

1. Report of the Board of Banking Supervision (Bank of England) Inquiry into the Circumstances of the Collapse of Barings, July 17, 1995. www.numa.com/ref/barings/bar00.htm

2. Trends in FDIC Professional Liability Litigation, Insights and Projections Based on the FDIC's First 27 Suits, NERA Economic Consulting, May 31, 2012. www.nera.com/nera-files/PUB_FDIC_Trends_0512.pdf

3. Characteristics of FDIC Lawsuits against Directors and Officers of Failed Financial Institutions, Cornerstone Research, May 2012. www.cornerstone.com/fdic_lawsuits_against_direct ors_and_officers/

4. Trepp Bank Failure Reports, Trepp, LLC. www.trepp.com/category/research/bank-failure-report/

5. GAO Report: Financial Institutions: Causes and Consequences of Recent Bank Failures, January 2013. http://www.gao.gov/assets/660/651154.pdf

6. OIG Report: Enforcement Actions and Professional Liability Claims Against Institution-Affiliated Parties and Individuals Associated with Failed Institutions, July 2014.

http://oig.federalreserve.gov/reports/board-actions-claims-failed-institutions-jul2014.pdf

Material Loss Reviews:

Federal law requires the study of certain bank failures by the Inspector General having jurisdiction over the failed bank. Prior to the enactment of the Dodd-Frank Act, Inspectors General were required to review the causes of an individual bank failure if the failure caused at least $25 million in losses to the Deposit Insurance Fund. Dodd-Frank generally limits such required reviews to those involving losses of at least $200 million if the losses occurred in 2010 or 2011, and at least $150 million from 2012 on.

Listed below is a link to each Inspector General website that will allow the reader to review all of the Material Loss Reviews.

Federal Reserve, Office of Inspector General
http://oig.federalreserve.gov/reports/audit-reports.htm

Federal Deposit Insurance Corporation, Office of Inspector General
http://www.fdicoig.gov/mlr.shtml

Office of the Comptroller of the Currency, Office of the Inspector General
www.treasury.gov/about/organizational-structure/ig/Pages/audit_reports_index.aspx

The American Association of Bank Directors has published a report entitled "What's Wrong with

Material Loss Reviews" which concludes that the methodology utilized by the Inspectors General is flawed, leading to flawed conclusions, and that the federal banking agencies (particularly the FDIC as receiver of failed banks reviewing MLRs to help determine whether to sue directors and officers) should not rely on the findings of the Material Loss Reviews for that reason.

APPENDIX II

FDIC LAW, REGULATIONS, RELATED ACTS

5000 - STATEMENT OF POLICY

Statement Concerning the Responsibilities of Bank Directors and Officers

The Federal Deposit Insurance Corporation is issuing this statement in response to concerns expressed by representatives of the banking industry and others regarding civil damage litigation risks to directors and officers of federally insured banks.

Duties of Directors and Officers

Service as a director or officer of a federally insured bank represents an important business assignment that carries with it commensurate duties and responsibilities.[1]

Banks need to be able to attract and to retain experienced and conscientious directors and officers. When an institution becomes troubled, it is especially important that it have the benefit of the advice and direction of people whose experience and talents enable them to exercise sound and prudent judgment.

Directors and officers of banks have obligations to discharge duties owed to their institution and to the shareholders and creditors of their institutions, and to comply with federal and state statutes, rules and regulations. Similar to the responsibilities owed by directors and officers of all business corporations, these duties include the duties of loyalty and care.

The duty of loyalty requires directors and officers to administer the affairs of the bank with candor, personal honesty and integrity. They are prohibited from advancing their own personal or business interests, or those of others, at the expense of the bank.

The duty of care requires directors and officers to act as prudent and diligent business persons in conducting the affairs of the bank.

This means that directors are responsible for selecting, monitoring, and evaluating competent management; establishing business strategies and policies; monitoring and assessing the progress of business operations; establishing and monitoring adherence to policies and procedures required by statute, regulation, and principles of safety and soundness; and for making business decisions on the basis of fully informed and meaningful deliberation.

Officers are responsible for running the day to day operations of the institution in compliance with applicable laws, rules, regulations and the principles of safety and soundness. This responsibility includes implementing appropriate policies and business objectives.

Directors must require and management must provide the directors with timely and ample information to discharge board responsibilities. Directors also are responsible for requiring management to respond promptly to supervisory criticism. Open and honest communication between the board and management of the bank and the regulator is extremely important.

The FDIC will not bring civil suits against directors and officers who fulfill their responsibilities, including the duties of loyalty and care, and who make reasonable business judgments on a fully informed basis and after proper deliberation.

Procedures Followed to Institute Civil Lawsuits

Lawsuits brought by the FDIC against former directors and officers of failed banks are instituted on the basis of detailed investigations conducted by the FDIC. Suits are not brought lightly or in haste.

The filing of such lawsuits is authorized only after a rigorous review of the factual circumstances surrounding the failure of the bank. In addition to review by senior FDIC supervisory and legal staff, all lawsuits against former directors and officers require final approval by the FDIC Board of Directors or designee.

In most cases, the FDIC attempts to alert proposed defendants in advance of filing lawsuits in order to permit them to respond to proposed charges informally and to discuss the prospect of pre-filing disposition or settlement of the proposed claims.

The FDIC brings suits only where they are believed to be sound on the merits and likely to be cost effective. On that basis, where investigations have been completed, the FDIC has brought suit (or settled claims) against former directors and officers with respect to 24% of the banks that have failed since 1985.

The FDIC's lawsuits are premised on the established legal principles that govern the conduct of directors and officers. Lawsuits against former directors and officers of failed banks result from a demonstrated failure to satisfy the duties of loyalty and care. Most suits involve evidence falling into at least one of the following categories:

- Cases where the director or officer engaged in dishonest conduct or approved or condoned abusive transactions with insiders.

- Cases where a director or officer was responsible for the failure of an institution to adhere to applicable laws and regulations, its own policies or an agreement with a supervisory authority, or where the director or officer otherwise participated in a safety or soundness violation.

- Cases where directors failed to establish proper underwriting policies and to monitor adherence thereto, or approved loans that they knew or had reason to know were improperly underwritten, or, in the case of outside directors, where the board failed to heed warnings from regulators or professional advisors, or where officers either failed to adhere to such policies or otherwise engaged in improper extensions of credit. Examples of improper underwriting have included lending to a borrower without obtaining adequate financial information, where the collateral was obviously inadequate, or where the borrower clearly lacked the ability to pay.

One factor considered in determining whether to bring an action against a director is the distinction between inside and outside directors. An inside director is generally an officer of the institution, or a member of a control group. An inside director generally has greater knowledge of and direct day to day responsibility for the management of the institution.

By contrast, an outside director usually has no connection to the bank other than his directorship and, perhaps, is a small or nominal shareholder. Outside directors generally do not participate in the conduct of the day to day business operations of the institution. The most common suits brought against outside directors either involve insider abuse or situations where the directors failed to heed warnings from regulators, accountants, attorneys or others that there was a significant problem in the bank which required correction. In the latter instance, if the directors fail to take steps to implement corrective measures, and the problem continued, the directors may be held liable for losses incurred after the warnings were given.

[Source: FDIC Financial Institution Letter (FIL--87--92) dated December 3, 1992]

[1]The regulatory agencies and others have produced guides that provide useful advice on ways directors can meet their duties to their institutions. These include the *Pocket Guide for Directors* (FDIC, 1988), *The Director's Book* (OCC, 1987), and FHLBB, Memorandum No. R 62, reprinted at 52 Fed. Reg. 22,682 (1987). See also *The Director's Guide: The Role and Responsibilities of a Savings Institution Director* (FHLB--SF, 1988).

APPENDIX III

AABD Letter to FDIC: Board Loan Approvals

**AMERICAN
ASSOCIATION
OF BANK DIRECTORS**

National Capital Office
Suite 700
1250 24ᵗʰ Street, NW
Washington, DC 20037
Telephone: (202) 463-4888
Facsimile: (202) 349-8080
www.aabd.org

June 23, 2011

The Honorable Sheila C. Bair
Chairman
Federal Deposit Insurance Corporation
550 17ᵗʰ Street, NW
Washington, DC 20429-9990

Dear Chairman Bair:

AABD recently advised bank directors to stop approving loans other than loans subject to Regulation O or involving certain insider conflicts. There are serious risks of potential personal liability that do not justify directors' involvement in the loan approval process unless the FDIC satisfactorily clarifies their appropriate role and corresponding personal liability. We ask that you direct the FDIC to clarify that role as soon as possible. A copy of my Viewpoint American Banker article dated June 14, 2011 is enclosed.

Large banks' boards and director loan committees commonly do not approve loans unless they are subject to Regulation O or internal insider transaction rules. Boards and director loan committees of community banks do commonly approve loans – often reserving their review and approval for the loans with the greatest amount of potential risk, such as large loans and loans that vary in some respect from loan policy.

Based on our review of FDIC complaints against directors of failed banks, we believe that a director's risk of personal liability is heightened by (i) voting for approval of loans; (ii) approving loans where the board or committee has received a board or committee loan package; or (iii) serving on a director loan committee. We are also aware of the FDIC's recent willingness to use its enforcement powers aggressively against directors of failed and open banks for "reckless lending."

A bank director's logical response to these suits and possible enforcement actions would be to do one of the following:

- Resign from the board
- Decline to serve on a director loan committee
- Decline to review or vote for approval of individual loans
- Only approve loans where there is no risk of repayment

Current federal laws, regulations and regulatory guidance do not require a board or board committee to approve any loans other than loans subject to Regulation O. So a board or board committee may choose simply not to be involved in the loan approval process. Directors may meet their fiduciary duties by adopting sound loan policies, procedures and controls, retaining a qualified CEO, relying reasonably on the CEO in assuring that other officers and employees of the Bank are qualified to do the kind of lending in which the Bank engages, monitoring adherence to loan policy and safe and sound lending practices, and taking steps to identify and correct any deficiencies in the lending process. Controls might include independent loan review and internal loan ratings, internal and outside audit of the lending function, and an independent credit function.

An alternative is for the board or board committee to approve only those loans that have no risk of repayment. Loans fully secured by certificates of deposit or by US bonds or notes could be approved, but unsecured loans or loans secured by real estate or other asset that can vary in value would not be.

AABD has advised its members not to approve loans until the FDIC formally clarifies its expectations and requirements for bank directors who want to be involved in the loan approval process.

We urge the FDIC to address the following questions:

- If a board or board committee decides not to be involved in the loan approval process at all (other than as to Regulation O and insider loan approvals under certain circumstances), what other measures, if any, will the FDIC expect the board or board committee to take in addition to the steps described in the first paragraph on page 2 of this letter?
- If a board or board committee relies on a board loan package in considering whether to approve loans, what should that loan package contain and what standards will the FDIC apply in determining whether a director who votes in favor of the loan is legally responsible for any statements or omissions in the board loan package?
- Does a bank director who serves on a director loan committee have a higher risk of being sued by the FDIC or being subject to an administrative action based on reckless lending than a bank director who does not serve on a director loan committee? If not, why is it that most of the complaints filed so far against directors of failed banks highlight that certain directors served on the director loan committee?

Sincerely,

David Baris
Executive Director

Enclosure

FDIC Response to AABD: Board Loan Approvals

Federal Deposit Insurance Corporation
550 17th Street NW, Washington, D.C. 20429-9990

General Counsel

August 1, 2011

Mr. David Baris
Executive Director
American Association of Bank Directors
National Capital Office
1250 24th Street, N.W., Suite 700
Washington, D.C. 20037

Dear Mr. Baris:

Thank you for your letter of June 23, 2011, to the Chairman. Your letter has been referred to me for a response.

You state in your letter that the American Association of Bank Directors ("AABD") "recently advised [community] bank directors to stop approving loans other than loans subject to Regulation O or involving certain insider conflicts." The basis of this advice is AABD's opinion, as also stated in your letter, that large banks' boards and loan committees commonly do not approve non-insider loans while boards and loan committees of community banks do approve such loans and that community bank directors' potential liability would be reduced if they were to stop approving non-insider loans. Your letter finally makes the somewhat disturbing statement that the AABD has advised its members not to approve loans until the FDIC clarifies its expectations and requirements.

The FDIC has not altered its expectations or requirements for bank directors and those standards have remained unchanged for many years. In short, bank directors owe duties of care and loyalty in fulfilling their responsibilities. The FDIC has only filed complaints against bank directors who failed to adhere to these long-standing standards. Consequently, there is no basis for your contentions that the standards require clarification or that the FDIC is imposing new requirements on bank directors that put them at risk of liability for appropriately performing their responsibilities. Bank directors are a critical component in the effective and efficient management of insured institutions precisely because they provide experience and community engagement that may not be otherwise found in bank management. We certainly do not believe it to be in the public's interest, or in the interest of the banking industry, for you to urge bank directors to avoid applying their experience and judgment to important credit decisions for the institution.

Directors of community banks typically approve larger non-insider loans on the merits either at the board or loan committee level. Given the relatively smaller size of a community bank compared to a money center bank, community bank directors are better able to supervise their smaller bank's lending function in this manner. Also as a result, members of community bank loan committees that are directors are in a better position to take prompt action to remedy observed weaknesses in their bank's lending function. Of course, a community bank, both as a legal and regulatory matter, may delegate loan approval authority below its loan committee if it so chooses, provided that the bank's board of directors amends the bank's loan policy to so provide. In fact, community banks often do delegate loan approval authority, at least for smaller non-insider loans, below the bank's loan

David Baris
July 28, 2011
Page 2

committee typically to lower level loan officers. If a bank were to do so for all non-insider loans, its loan committee members, whether directors or officers, would no longer have the responsibility to approve non-insider loans on the merits. While this may not be a best practice from the standpoint of good corporate governance for the reasons noted, it is not legally prohibited.

If authority is delegated to lower level officers in the bank's organization, the board of directors nevertheless would retain its nondelegable duty to supervise the bank's lending function. Directors cannot delegate their ultimate responsibility to supervise the core functions of the bank. Directors of financial institutions, large or small, are responsible for establishing the strategic direction of the bank, including managing risks and supervising management to ensure that strategic goals are met. This requires bank directors to undertake diligent and ongoing review of information concerning the bank's operations and performance, including – specifically with respect to the loan approval function – information and data on credit and other risks, loan concentrations, incentive compensation to make loans, and compliance with loan policies, statutes, and regulations, among other things.

If, however, a bank's board has delegated authority to approve non-insider loans to a loan committee, the loan committee members cannot abdicate their responsibility and instead must review loan files and either approve or refuse extensions of credit in accordance with applicable loan policies and safe and sound underwriting standards. If the committee members fail to do so, they risk legal liability that is very well-established by law. If, as is typically the case, the loan committee relies on loan packages to approve loans, the packages must be sufficiently detailed to enable the committee members to make informed and sound business judgments on the merits of the loans that they are approving or rejecting.

The final point in your letter is that over the past year the FDIC has filed several complaints against community bank directors (and officers in some cases) for breaching their duties as members of the failed bank's loan committee. In these cases, the loan committee members had been delegated the authority to approve the loss loans at issue by their boards of directors, but they breached their duties of care, and in some cases their duties of loyalty, to the bank when they approved loans that violated the bank's loan policy and underwriting standards, among other things, and in some instances that were abusive insider transactions.

I am confident that community bank directors will keep these well-established corporate governance and legal banking principles firmly in mind as they reflect on the AABD's recent advice. Thank you again for your June 23 letter to the Chairman. If you have any questions regarding anything in this letter, please feel free to contact me or Richard J. Osterman, Jr., Deputy General Counsel, at (202) 898-3706.

Sincerely,

Michael Krimminger
General Counsel

ACKNOWLEDGEMENTS

I wish to thank my co-author, Loyal Horsley, who assisted in the update to the Second Edition of this Report, and Jared Kelly, who wrote drafts of the First Edition of the Report and provided valuable research and review. I also would like to thank Charles Thayer, Chairman Emeritus of AABD, Robert Ambler and Jamie Connelly of Womble Carlyle, and Aaron Mahler of BuckleySandler for their substantial contributions to the First Edition of the Report.

David Baris, President
American Association of Bank Directors

DAVID BARIS

David Baris, President of the American Association of Bank Directors, helped found AABD, a non-profit trade association, in 1989 to represent the interests of individual bank directors in the midst of the S&L crisis.

AABD provides bank directors with the resources to serve their institutions effectively and in a manner that will minimize risk of personal liability, and represents their interests before federal and state legislative bodies, banking supervisory agencies and judicial bodies.

Baris is a partner in the Washington, DC office of BuckleySandler LLP. He represents financial institutions throughout the United States on securities, corporate, transactional, and regulatory matters. Baris has more than 30 years' experience advising financial institutions on a variety of matters.

Baris was a director of Mutual of Omaha Insurance Co. and United of Omaha Life Insurance Co. from 2000 to 2004, serving on their executive, audit, and investment committees.

LOYAL HORSLEY

Loyal Horsley, formerly a Law Clerk to the American Association of Bank Directors, is an associate in the Washington, DC office of BuckleySandler LLP.

AMERICAN ASSOCIATION OF BANK DIRECTORS

Founded in 1989 in the midst of the S&L crisis, the nonprofit American Association of Bank Directors (AABD) is devoted to serving the information, education, and advocacy needs of individual bank and savings institution directors.

Bank regulators expect bank and savings institution boards of directors to make informed decisions and to act independently to supervise their institution. One way for CEOs and their boards of directors to demonstrate that their boards are both informed and independent is through membership in AABD – the only banking trade association in the United States which exclusively serves individual directors rather than their institutions.

Bank directors are overburdened, often undercompensated, and under undue threat of personal liability. AABD advocates changes in banking laws and banking agency regulations, regulatory guidance, examinations, and practices that will allow bank directors to better meet their fiduciary duties without being subject to excessive regulatory burdens and unjustified risk of personal liability.

Advocacy: AABD reviews and responds to legislative and regulatory actions that impact bank directors. The Second Edition of the Bank Director Regulatory Burden Study, issued in 2014, is a special report that recommends that the federal banking agencies and the U.S. Congress take steps to reduce the huge regulatory burdens imposed on bank directors.

Education: AABD encourages all bank directors to participate in AABD's Bank Director Certification Program, which enables bank directors to obtain formal training on their duties and responsibilities and on oversight of lending, investments, ALCO, risk management, liquidity, audit, compensation and other relevant topics. AmTrust, a D&O carrier, offers credits of up to 15% on premiums paid by banks whose directors participate in the Bank Director Certification Program.

Information Resources: AABD acts as a central clearinghouse, identifying important resources for AABD members, from bank regulators, the U.S. Congress, national and state banking associations, banking publications and AABD sponsors. AABD provides analysis of developments affecting bank directors.

Banks whose directors are AABD Premium Members receive a complimentary copy of all AABD special reports and publications.

www.AABD.org

21097073R00193

Made in the USA
Middletown, DE
19 June 2015